To

From

Date

Values
for Life

WALNUT GROVE PRESS
Nashville, TN 37202

The quoted ideas expressed in this book (but not scripture verses) are not, in all cases, exact quotations, as some have been edited for clarity and brevity. In all cases, the author has attempted to maintain the speaker's original intent. In some cases, quoted material for this book was obtained from secondary sources, primarily print media. While every effort was made to ensure the accuracy of these sources, the accuracy cannot be guaranteed. For additions, deletions, corrections or clarifications in future editions of this text, please write WALNUT GROVE PRESS.

Cover Design by Kim Russell / Wahoo Designs
Page Layout by Bart Dawson

ISBN 1-58334-251-6

Printed in the United States of America

Values
for Life

Timeless Wisdom
for Godly Living

FCP
FAMILY
CHRISTIAN
PRESS

In all your ways acknowledge Him, and He shall direct your paths.

Proverbs 3:6 NKJV

Table of Contents

Introduction

How many decisions do you make in a typical day? When you stop to think about it, you make thousands of choices, usually without too much forethought. Of course, most of these choices are relatively small ones, like what to do at a given moment or what to say or how to direct your thoughts. Occasionally, you will face major decisions, like choosing to be a Christian or choosing a profession or choosing a spouse. But whatever choices you face—whether they're big, little, or somewhere in between—you can be sure of this: the quality of your choices will make an enormous difference in the quality of your life.

Your choices are shaped by your values. Simply put, your values determine, to a surprising extent, the quality of the decisions you make *and* the direction that your life will take. And that's why the ideas in this book are so important.

This book addresses Christian values that can—and should—shape your life. You may find it helpful to read the book from cover to cover, or you may decide to scan the Table of Contents and then turn to chapters that seem particularly important to you. Either way, the ideas on these pages will serve to remind you of God's commandments, God's promises, God's love, and God's Son—all things that are crucially important as you establish priorities for the next stage of your life's journey.

Whose values do you hold most dear: society's values or God's values? When you decide to make God's priorities your priorities, you will receive His abundance and His peace. When you make God a full partner in every aspect of your life, He will lead you along the proper path: His path. When you allow God to direct your steps, He will honor you with spiritual blessings that are simply too numerous to count. So, as you make your next important decision, pause to consider the values that serve as the starting point for that decision. When you do, your decision-making will be vastly improved . . . and so will your life.

The Lord says, "I will make you wise and show you where to go.
I will guide you and watch over you."

Psalm 32:8 NCV

Values for Life

And I pray this: that your love will keep on growing in knowledge and every kind of discernment, so that you can determine what really matters and can be pure and blameless in the day of Christ.

Philippians 1:9 HCSB

Whether you realize it or not, your life is shaped by your values. From the time you wake up in the morning until the moment you drift off to sleep at night, your actions are guided by the values that you hold most dear. If you're a thoughtful believer, those values are shaped by the Word of God.

Society seeks to impose its set of values upon you; however, these values are often contrary to God's Word and, thus, to your own best interests. The world makes promises that it simply cannot fulfill. It promises happiness, contentment, prosperity, and abundance. But genuine abundance is not a byproduct of possessions or status; it is a byproduct of your thoughts, your actions, and your relationship with God. The world's promises are incomplete and illusory; God's promises are unfailing. Your challenge, then, is to build your value system upon the firm foundation of God's promises . . . nothing else will suffice.

Each day, you make countless decisions, decisions that hopefully can bring you into a closer relationship with your Heavenly Father. When God's values become your values, then you share in His abundance and His peace. But, if you place the world's priorities above God's priorities, then you will, in time, suffer the consequences of your shortsightedness.

As a citizen of the 21st century, you live in a world that is filled with countless opportunities to stray from God's will. The world seems to cry, "Worship me with your time, your money, your energy, and your thoughts!" But God commands otherwise: He commands you to worship Him and Him alone; everything else must be secondary.

Do you seek God's peace and His blessings? Then build your life upon a value system that puts God first. When you're faced with a difficult choice or a powerful temptation, seek God's counsel and trust the counsel that He gives. Invite God into your heart and live according to His commandments. Study His Word and talk to Him often. When you do, you will share in the abundance and peace that only God can give.

If you want to be proactive in the way you live your life, if you want to influence your life's direction, if you want your life to exhibit the qualities you find desireable, and if you want to live with integrity, then you need to know what your values are, decide to embrace them, and practice them every day.

John Maxwell

Values for Life

Whose values? You can have the values that the world holds dear, or you can have the values that God holds dear, but you can't have both. The decision is yours . . . and so are the consequences.

Timeless Wisdom for Godly Living

I may no longer depend on pleasant impulses to bring me before the Lord. I must rather respond to principles I know to be right, whether I feel them to be enjoyable or not.

Jim Elliot

Only grief and disappointment can result from continued violation of the divine principles that underlie the spiritual life.

A. W. Tozer

But also for this very reason, giving all diligence, add to your faith virtue, to virtue knowledge.

2 Peter 1:5 NKJV

The world has never been stable. Jesus Himself was born into the cruelest and most unstable of worlds. No, we have babies and keep trusting and living because the Resurrection is true! The Resurrection was not just a one-time event in history; it is a principle built into the very fabric of our beings, a fact reverberating from every cell of creation: Life wins! Life wins!

Gloria Gaither

Human worth does not depend on beauty or intelligence or accomplishments. We are all more valuable than the possessions of the entire world simply because God gave us that value.

James Dobson

More Words from God's Word

Be on guard. Stand true to what you believe. Be courageous. Be strong.

1 Corinthians 16:13 NLT

But what happens when we live God's way? He brings gifts into our lives, much the same way that fruit appears in an orchard, things like affection for others, exuberance about life, serenity. We develop a willingness to stick with things, a sense of compassion in the heart, and a conviction that a basic holiness permeates things and people. We find ourselves involved in loyal commitments, not needing to force our way in life, able to marshal and direct our energies wisely.

Galatians 5:22-23 MSG

Finally, brethren, whatever things are true, whatever things are noble, whatever things are just, whatever things are pure, whatever things are lovely, whatever things are of good report, if there is any virtue and if there is anything praiseworthy—meditate on these things.

Philippians 4:8 NKJV

My Values for Life

	Check Your Value		
	High	Med.	Low
The importance that I place upon living a principled life . . .	___	___	___
The value of studying God's Word and living by it . . .	___	___	___
The importance that I place upon sharing my value system with family and friends . . .	___	___	___

Wisdom According to Whom?

*But the wisdom that is from above is first pure,
then peaceable, gentle, willing to yield, full of mercy and good fruits,
without partiality and without hypocrisy.*

James 3:17 NKJV

Do you place a high value on the acquisition of wisdom? If so, you are not alone; most people would like to be wise, but not everyone is willing to do the work that is required to become wise. Wisdom is not like a mushroom; it does not spring up overnight. It is, instead, like an oak tree that starts as a tiny acorn, grows into a sapling, and eventually reaches up to the sky, tall and strong.

To become wise, you must seek God's guidance and live according to His Word. To become wise, you must seek instruction with consistency and purpose. To become wise, you must not only learn the lessons of the Christian life, you must also live by them. But oftentimes, that's easier said than done.

Sometimes, amid the demands of daily life, you will lose perspective. Life may seem out of balance, and the pressures of everyday living may seem overwhelming. What's needed is a fresh perspective, a restored sense of balance . . . and God's wisdom. If you call upon the Lord and seek to see the world through His eyes, He will give you guidance, wisdom, and perspective. When you make God's priorities your priorities, He will lead you according to His plan and according to His commandments. When you study God's teachings, you are reminded that God's reality is the ultimate reality.

Do you seek to live a life of righteousness and wisdom? If so, you must study the ultimate source of wisdom: the Word of God. You must seek out worthy mentors and listen carefully to their advice. You must associate, day in and day out, with godly men and women. Then, as you accumulate wisdom, you must not keep it for yourself; you must, instead, share it with your friends and family members.

But be forewarned: if you sincerely seek to share your hard-earned wisdom with others, your actions must reflect the values that you hold dear. The best way to share your wisdom—perhaps the only way—is not by your words but by your example.

Wise people listen to wise instruction,
especially instruction from the Word of God.

Warren Wiersbe

Values for Life

Need wisdom? God's got it. If you want it, then study God's Word and associate with godly people.

Timeless Wisdom for Godly Living

Having a doctrine pass before the mind is not what the Bible means by knowing the truth. It's only when it reaches down deep into the heart that the truth begins to set us free, just as a key must penetrate a lock to turn it, or as rainfall must saturate the earth down to the roots in order for your garden to grow.

John Eldredge

The fruit of wisdom is Christlikeness, peace, humility, and love. And, the root of it is faith in Christ as the manifested wisdom of God.

J. I. Packer

Wisdom is the God-given ability to see life with rare objectivity and to handle life with rare stability.

Charles Swindoll

Those who are wise will shine like the brightness of the heavens, and those who lead many to righteousness, like the stars for ever and ever.

Daniel 12:3 NIV

Wisdom is knowledge applied.
Head knowledge is useless on the battlefield.
Knowledge stamped on the heart makes one wise.

Beth Moore

More Words from God's Word

Every morning he wakes me. He teaches me to listen like a student. The Lord God helps me learn . . .

Isaiah 50:4-5 NCV

Let the word of Christ dwell in you richly in all wisdom; teaching and admonishing one another in psalms and hymns and spiritual songs, singing with grace in your hearts to the Lord.

Colossians 3:16 KJV

But also for this very reason, giving all diligence, add to your faith virtue, to virtue knowledge.

2 Peter 1:5 NKJV

Therefore everyone who hears these words of mine and puts them into practice is like a wise man who built his house on the rock.

Matthew 7:24 NIV

My Values for Life

For me, the acquisition of wisdom has . . .

Associating myself with wise friends has . . .

The importance that I place upon behaving wisely and obediently . . .

Check Your Value		
High	Med.	Low
___	___	___
___	___	___
___	___	___

Where Do I Spend My Time?

So teach us to number our days, that we may gain a heart of wisdom.
Psalm 90:12 NKJV

Do you place a high value on your time? Hopefully you do. After all, time is a precious, nonrenewable gift from God. But sometimes, amid the complications of life here in the 21st century, you will be sorely tempted to squander the time that God has given you. Why? Because you live in a society filled to the brim with powerful temptations and countless distractions, all of which take time.

An important element of your stewardship to God is the way that you choose to spend the time He has entrusted to you. Each waking moment holds the potential to help a friend or aid a stranger, to say a kind word or think a noble thought or offer a heartfelt prayer. Your challenge, as a believer, is to value your time, to use it judiciously, and to use it in ways that honor your Heavenly Father.

As you establish priorities for your day and your life, remember that each new day is a special treasure to be savored and celebrated. As a Christian, you have much to celebrate and much to do. It's up to you, and you alone, to honor God for the gift of time by using that gift wisely. Every day, like every life, is composed of moments. Each moment of your life holds within it the potential to seek God's will and to serve His purposes. If you are wise, you will strive to do both.

How will you invest your time today? Will you savor the moments of your life, or will you squander them? Will you use your time as an instrument of God's will, or will you allow commonplace distractions to rule your day and your life?

The gift of time is indeed a gift from God. Treat it as if it were a precious, fleeting, one-of-a-kind treasure. Because it is.

Our time is short!
The time we can invest for God, in creative things,
in receiving our fellowmen for Christ, is short!

Billy Graham

Values for Life

If you don't value your time . . . neither will anybody else.

Timeless Wisdom for Godly Living

The more time you give to something,
the more you reveal its importance and value to you.

Rick Warren

God has a present will for your life.
It is neither chaotic nor utterly exhausting.
In the midst of many good choices vying for your time,
He will give you the discernment to recognize what is best.

Beth Moore

Frustration is not the will of God.
There is time to do anything and everything that God wants us to do.

Elisabeth Elliot

To choose time is to save time.

Francis Bacon

Overcommitment and time pressures are the greatest destroyers
of marriages and families. It takes time to develop any friendship,
whether with a loved one or with God himself.

James Dobson

To everything there is a season,
a time for every purpose under heaven.

Ecclesiastes 3:1 NKJV

More Words from God's Word

Lord, tell me when the end will come and how long I will live.
Let me know how long I have. You have given me only a short life;
my lifetime is like nothing to you. Everyone's life is only a breath.

Psalm 39:4-5 NCV

For he says, "In the time of my favor I heard you, and in the day of salvation I helped you." I tell you, now is the time of God's favor, now is the day of salvation.

2 Corinthians 6:2 NIV

While it is daytime, we must continue doing the work of the One who sent me. Night is coming, when no one can work.

John 9:4 NCV

Give your entire attention to what God is doing right now, and don't get worked up about what may or may not happen tomorrow. God will help you deal with whatever hard things come up when the time comes.

Matthew 6:34 MSG

My Values for Life

	Check Your Value		
	High	Med.	Low
For me, the need to prioritize my day is . . .	___	___	___
Time spent with my family is . . .	___	___	___
Time spent in worship, prayer, or Bible study is . . .	___	___	___

Stupendously Blessed

Therefore, since we receive a kingdom which cannot be shaken, let us show gratitude, by which we may offer to God an acceptable service with reverence and awe . . . .

Hebrews 12:28 NASB

As believers who have been touched by God's grace, we are blessed beyond measure. God sent His only Son to die for our sins. And, God has given us the priceless gifts of eternal love and eternal life. We, in turn, are instructed to approach our Heavenly Father with reverence and thanksgiving. But, as busy people caught up in the inevitable demands of everyday life, we sometimes fail to pause and thank our Creator for the countless blessings that He has bestowed upon us.

Sometimes life is complicated; sometimes life is frustrating; and sometimes life is downright exhausting. When the demands of life leave us rushing from place to place with scarcely a moment to spare, we may fail to pause and thank our Creator for His gifts. Yet whenever we neglect to give proper thanks to the Giver of all things good, we suffer because of our misplaced priorities.

The words of 1 Thessalonians 5:18 remind us to give thanks in every circumstance of life: "In everything give thanks; for this is the will of God in Christ Jesus for you" (NKJV). But sometimes, when our hearts are troubled and our lives seem to be spinning out of control, we don't feel like thanking anybody, including our Father in heaven. Yet God's Word is clear: In all circumstances, our Creator offers us His love, His strength, and His grace. And in all circumstances, we must thank Him.

Thoughtful believers (like you) see the need to praise God with sincerity, with humility, and with consistency. So whatever your circumstances—even if you are overworked, overcommitted, and overstressed—slow down and express your thanks to the Creator. When you do, you'll discover that your expressions of gratitude will enrich your own life as well as the lives of your loved ones.

Thanksgiving should become a habit, a regular part of your daily routine. After all, God has blessed you beyond measure, and you owe Him everything, including your eternal gratitude . . . starting now.

It is only with gratitude that life becomes rich.

Dietrich Bonhoeffer

Values for Life

Two Magic Words: Thank you! People never become tired of hearing those two little words, and neither, for that matter, does God.

Timeless Wisdom for Godly Living

It is always possible to be thankful for what is given rather
than to complain about what is not given.
One or the other becomes a habit of life.

Elisabeth Elliot

Thanksgiving is good but Thanksliving is better.

Jim Gallery

The act of thanksgiving is a demonstration of the fact
that you are going to trust and believe God.

Kay Arthur

*Everything created by God is good, and nothing
is to be rejected, if it is received with gratitude;
for it is sanctified by means of the word of God and prayer.*

1 Timothy 4:4-5 NASB

The devil moves in when a Christian starts to complain,
but thanksgiving in the Spirit defeats the devil and glorifies the Lord.

Warren Wiersbe

God is worthy of our praise and is pleased
when we come before Him with thanksgiving.

Shirley Dobson

Gratitude

More Words from God's Word

As you therefore have received Christ Jesus the Lord, so walk in Him, having been firmly rooted and now being built up in Him and established in your faith, just as you were instructed, and overflowing with gratitude.

Colossians 2:6-7 NASB

Enter his gates with thanksgiving, go into his courts with praise.
Give thanks to him and bless his name.

Psalm 100:4 NLT

It is good to give thanks to the LORD, to sing praises to the Most High.
It is good to proclaim your unfailing love in the morning,
your faithfulness in the evening.

Psalm 92:1-2 NLT

I will give thanks to the LORD with all my heart;
I will tell of all Your wonders. I will be glad and exult in You;
I will sing praise to Your name, O Most High.

Psalm 9:1-2 NASB

My Values for Life

	Check Your Value		
	High	Med.	Low
The importance that I place upon thanking God for His gifts . . .	___	___	___
The value of searching for opportunities not problems . . .	___	___	___
The value of thanking God for His perfect plan even when I don't understand that plan . . .	___	___	___

With God as Your Partner

Until now you have not asked for anything in my name. Ask and you will receive, so that your joy will be the fullest possible joy.

John 16:24 NCV

How often do you ask God for His help and His wisdom? Occasionally? Intermittently? Whenever you experience a crisis? Hopefully not. Hopefully, you've acquired the habit of asking for God's assistance early and often. And hopefully, you have learned to seek His guidance in every aspect of your life.

Jesus made it clear to His disciples: they should petition God to meet their needs. So should you. Genuine, heartfelt prayer produces powerful changes in you and in your world. When you lift your heart to God, you open yourself to a never-ending source of divine wisdom and infinite love.

James 5:16 makes a promise that God intends to keep: when you pray earnestly, fervently, and often, great things will happen. Too many people, however, are too timid or too pessimistic to ask God to do big things. Please don't count yourself among their number.

God can do great things through you if you have the courage to ask Him (and the determination to keep asking Him). But don't expect Him to do all the work. When you do your part, He will do His part—and when He does, you can expect miracles to happen.

The Bible promises that God will guide you if you let Him.

Your job is to let Him. But sometimes, you will be tempted to do otherwise. Sometimes, you'll be tempted to go along with the crowd; other times, you'll be tempted to do things your way not God's way. When you feel those temptations, resist them.

God has promised that when you ask for His help, He will not withhold it. So ask. Ask Him to meet the needs of your day. Ask Him to lead you, to protect you, and to correct you. Then, trust the answers He gives.

God stands at the door and waits. When you knock, He opens. When you ask, He answers. Your task, of course, is to make God a full partner in every aspect of your life—and to seek His guidance prayerfully, confidently, and often.

We honor God by asking for great things when they are a part of His promise. We dishonor Him and cheat ourselves when we ask for molehills where He has promised mountains.

Vance Havner

Values for Life

Pray early and often. One way to make sure that your heart is in tune with God is to pray often. The more you talk to God, the more He will talk to you.

Timeless Wisdom for Godly Living

We get into trouble when we think we *know* what to do and we stop *asking* God if we're doing it.

Stormie Omartian

By asking in Jesus' name, we're making a request not only in His authority, but also for His interests and His benefit.

Shirley Dobson

Do not worry about anything, but pray and ask God for everything you need, always giving thanks.

Philippians 4:6 NCV

God's help is always available, but it is only given to those who seek it.

Max Lucado

Notice that we must ask. And we will sometimes struggle to hear and struggle with what we hear. But personally, it's worth it. I'm after the path of life—and he alone knows it.

John Eldredge

God will help us become the people we are meant to be, if only we will ask Him.

Hannah Whitall Smith

More Words from God's Word

*Ask and it will be given to you; seek and you will find;
knock and the door will be opened to you. For everyone who asks receives;
he who seeks finds; and to him who knocks, the door will be opened.*

Matthew 7:7-8 NIV

*You did not choose me, but I chose you and appointed you to go
and bear fruit—fruit that will last.
Then the Father will give you whatever you ask in my name.*

John 15:16 NIV

*Verily, verily, I say unto you, He that believeth on me, the works that
I do shall he do also; and greater works than these shall he do;
because I go unto my Father. And whatsoever ye shall ask in my name,
that will I do, that the Father may be glorified in the Son.
If ye shall ask any thing in my name, I will do it.*

John 14:12-14 KJV

My Values for Life

	Check Your Value		
	High	Med.	Low
The importance that I place upon talking to God . . .	___	___	___
The importance of spending quiet time listening to God . . .	___	___	___
The importance of making God a partner in every aspect of my life . . .	___	___	___

The Power of Purpose

You will show me the path of life; in Your presence is fullness of joy; at Your right hand are pleasures forevermore.

Psalm 16:11 NKJV

Life is best lived on purpose not by accident: the sooner we discover what God intends for us to do with our lives, the better. But God's purposes aren't always clear to us. Sometimes we wander aimlessly in a wilderness of our own making. And sometimes, we struggle mightily against God in a vain effort to find success and happiness through our own means not His.

Whenever we struggle against God's plans, we suffer. When we resist God's calling, our efforts bear little fruit. Our best strategy, therefore, is to seek God's wisdom and to follow Him wherever He chooses to lead. When we do so, we are blessed.

When we align ourselves with God's purposes, we avail ourselves of His power and His peace. But how can we know precisely what God's intentions are? The answer, of course, is that even the most well-intentioned believers face periods of uncertainty and doubt about the direction of their lives. So, too, will you.

When you arrive at one of life's inevitable crossroads, that is precisely the moment when you should turn your thoughts and prayers toward God. When you do, He will make Himself known to you in a time and manner of His choosing.

Are you earnestly seeking to discern God's purpose for your life? If so, remember this:

1. God has a plan for your life;

2. If you seek that plan sincerely and prayerfully, you will find it;

3. When you discover God's purpose for your life, you will experience abundance, peace, joy, and power—God's power. And that's the only kind of power that really matters.

His life is our light—our purpose and meaning and reason for living.

Anne Graham Lotz

Values for Life

Discovering God's purpose for your life requires a willingness to be open. God's plan is unfolding day by day. If you keep your eyes and your heart open, He'll reveal His plans. God has big things in store for you, but He may have quite a few lessons to teach you before you are fully prepared to do His will and fulfill His purposes.

Timeless Wisdom for Godly Living

It's incredible to realize that what we do each day has meaning
in the big picture of God's plan.

Bill Hybels

We aren't just thrown on this earth like dice tossed across a table.
We are lovingly placed here for a purpose.

Charles Swindoll

The promise of Psalm 121 is not that we shall never stub our toes,
but that no injury, no illness, no accident, no distress
will have evil power over us, that is, will be able
to separate us from God's purposes in us.

Eugene Peterson

The Christian life is not simply following principles but being
empowered to fulfill our purpose: knowing and exalting Christ.

Franklin Graham

To everything there is a season,
a time for every purpose under heaven.

Ecclesiastes 3:1 NKJV

We are most vulnerable to the piercing winds of doubt when
we distance ourselves from the mission and fellowship to which
Christ has called us.

Joni Eareckson Tada

More Words from God's Word

*God chose you to be his people,
so I urge you now to live the life to which God called you.*

Ephesians 4:1 NCV

*There is one thing I always do. Forgetting the past and straining
toward what is ahead, I keep trying to reach the goal
and get the prize for which God called me . . . .*

Philippians 3:13-14 NCV

*May He grant you according to your heart's desire,
and fulfill all your purpose.*

Psalm 20:4 NKJV

*We know that all things work together for the good of those who love God:
those who are called according to His purpose.*

Romans 8:28 HCSB

My Values for Life

	Check Your Value		
	High	Med.	Low
I consider my personal search for purpose and meaning to be . . .	___	___	___
For me, prayerfully petitioning God has . . .	___	___	___
Trusting God to reveal His plans for my life is a priority that has . . .	___	___	___

Making Forgiveness a High Priority

And be kind to one another, tenderhearted, forgiving one another, just as God in Christ forgave you.

Ephesians 4:32 NKJV

Do you value the role that forgiveness can play in your life? Hopefully so. But even if you're a dedicated believer, you may have a difficult time forgiving those who have hurt you. If you're one of those folks who, despite your best intentions, has a difficult time forgiving and forgetting, you are not alone.

Life would be much simpler if we humans could forgive people "once and for all" and be done with it. But forgiveness is seldom that easy. For most people, the decision to forgive is straightforward, but the process of forgiving is more difficult. Forgiveness is a journey that requires effort, time, perseverance, and prayer.

Sometimes, it's not "the other person" whom you need to forgive; it's yourself. If you've made mistakes (and who among us hasn't?), perhaps you're continuing to bear a grudge against the person in the mirror. If so, here's a three-step process for resolving those feelings:

1. Stop the harmful behavior that is the source of your self-directed anger.
2. Seek forgiveness from God (and from any people whom you may have hurt).

3. Ask God to cleanse your heart of all bitterness and regret . . . and keep asking Him until your feelings of anger and regret are gone.

If there exists even one person, alive or dead, whom you have not forgiven (and that includes yourself), follow God's commandment: forgive that person today. And remember that bitterness, anger, and regret are not part of God's plan for your life. Forgiveness is.

Perhaps you need a refresher course in the art of forgiveness. If so, it's time to open your Bible *and* your heart. When you do, you'll discover that God can heal your broken spirit. Don't expect forgiveness to be easy or quick, but rest assured that with God as your partner, you can forgive . . . and *you will.*

Learning how to forgive and forget is one of the secrets of a happy Christian life.

Warren Wiersbe

Values for Life

Forgive . . . and keep forgiving! Sometimes, you may forgive someone once and then, at a later time, become angry at the very same person again. If so, you must forgive that person again and again . . . until it sticks!

Timeless Wisdom for Godly Living

Forgiveness is actually the best revenge because it not only sets us free from the person we forgive, but it frees us to move into all that God has in store for us.

Stormie Omartian

Two works of mercy set a man free: forgive and you will be forgiven, and give and you will receive.

St. Augustine

There are some facts that will never change.
One fact is that you are forgiven. He sees you
better than you see yourself. And that is a glorious fact of your life.

Max Lucado

How often should you forgive the other person?
Only as many times as you want God to forgive you!

Marie T. Freeman

When you harbor bitterness, happiness will dock elsewhere.

Anonymous

Stop judging others, and you will not be judged.
Stop criticizing others, or it will all come back on you.
If you forgive others, you will be forgiven.

Luke 6:37 NLT

More Words from God's Word

You have heard that it was said, "Love your neighbor and hate your enemy." But I tell you: Love your enemies and pray for those who persecute you.

Matthew 5:43-44 NIV

Those who show mercy to others are happy, because God will show mercy to them.

Matthew 5:7 NCV

If someone does wrong to you, do not pay him back by doing wrong to him. Try to do what everyone thinks is right.

Romans 12:17 NCV

And whenever you stand praying, if you have anything against anyone, forgive him, so that your Father in heaven may also forgive you your wrongdoing.

Mark 11:25 HCSB

My Values for Life

	Check Your Value		
	High	Med.	Low
For me, forgiveness is not optional; it is a commandment from God . . .	___	___	___
I consider forgiveness to be a way of liberating myself from the chains of the past . . .	___	___	___
Forgiving other people is one way of strengthening my relationship with God . . .	___	___	___

The Value of Worship

Worship the Lord your God and . . . serve Him only.

Matthew 4:10 HCSB

All of humanity is engaged in worship. The question is not whether we worship but what we worship. Wise men and women choose to worship God. When they do, they are blessed with a plentiful harvest of joy, peace, and abundance. Other people choose to distance themselves from God by foolishly worshipping things that are intended to bring personal gratification but not spiritual gratification. Such choices often have tragic consequences.

If we place our love for material possessions above our love for God—or if we yield to the countless temptations of this world—we find ourselves engaged in a struggle between good and evil, a clash between God and Satan. Our responses to these struggles have implications that echo throughout our families and throughout our communities.

How can we ensure that we cast our lot with God? We do so, in part, by the practice of regular, purposeful worship in the company of fellow believers. When we worship God faithfully and fervently, we are blessed. When we fail to worship God, for whatever reason, we forfeit the spiritual gifts that He intends for us.

We must worship our Heavenly Father not only with our words but also with deeds. We must honor Him, praise Him, and obey Him. As we seek to find purpose and meaning for our lives, we must first seek His purpose and His will. For believers, God comes first. Always first.

Do you place a high value on the practice of worship? Hopefully so. After all, every day provides countless opportunities to put God where He belongs: at the very center of your life. It's up to you to worship God seven days a week; anything less is simply not enough.

I am of the opinion that we should not be concerned about working for God until we have learned the meaning and delight of worshipping Him.

A. W. Tozer

Values for Life

Worship is not meant to be boxed up in a church building on Sunday morning. To the contrary, praise and worship should be woven into the very fabric of your day. Do you take time each day to worship your Father in heaven, or do you wait until Sunday morning to praise Him for His blessings? The answer to this question will, in large part, determine the quality and direction of your life. So worship accordingly.

Timeless Wisdom for Godly Living

Each time, before you intercede, be quiet first and worship
God in His glory. Think of what He can do and how He delights
to hear the prayers of His redeemed people.
Think of your place and privilege in Christ, and expect great things!

Andrew Murray

*A time is coming and has now come when
the true worshipers will worship the Father in spirit and
truth, for they are the kind of worshipers the Father seeks.
God is spirit, and his worshipers must
worship in spirit and in truth.*

John 4:23-24 NIV

God asks that we worship Him with our concentrated minds
as well as with our wills and emotions.
A divided and scattered mind is not effective.

Catherine Marshall

It is impossible to worship God and remain unchanged.

Henry Blackaby

Worship is not taught from the pulpit. It must be learned in the heart.

Jim Elliot

More Words from God's Word

Shout with joy to the LORD, O earth!
Worship the LORD with gladness. Come before him, singing with joy.

Psalm 100:1-2 NLT

God lifted him high and honored him far beyond anyone or anything, ever, so that all created beings in heaven and earth, even those long ago dead and buried, will bow in worship before this Jesus Christ, and call out in praise that he is the Master of all, to the glorious honor of God the Father.

Philippians 2:9-11 MSG

All the earth shall worship thee, and shall sing unto thee;
they shall sing to thy name . . . .

Psalm 66:4 KJV

Happy are those who hear the joyful call to worship,
for they will walk in the light of your presence, LORD.

Psalm 89:15 NLT

My Values for Life

Statement	Check Your Value: High	Med.	Low
The value that I place on the practice of regular worship is . . .	___	___	___
For me, worshipping with fellow believers has benefits that are . . .	___	___	___
Worshipping God gives me a sense of comfort and a sense of direction that is . . .	___	___	___

A Humble Heart

Do nothing out of rivalry or conceit,
but in humility consider others as more important than yourselves.

Philippians 2:3 HCSB

We have heard the phrases on countless occasions: "He's a self-made man," or "she's a self-made woman." In truth, none of us are self-made. We all owe countless debts that we can never repay.

Our first debt, of course, is to our Father in heaven—Who has given us everything—and to His Son Who sacrificed His own life so that we might live eternally. We are also indebted to ancestors, parents, teachers, friends, spouses, family members, coworkers, fellow believers . . . and the list, of course, goes on.

As Christians, we have a profound reason to be humble: We have been refashioned and saved by Jesus Christ, and that salvation came not because of our own good works but because of God's grace. Thus, we are not "self-made"; we are "God-made," and "Christ-saved." How, then, can we be boastful? The answer, of course, is that, if we are honest with ourselves and with our God, we simply can't be boastful... we must, instead, be eternally grateful and exceedingly humble.

Humility is not, in most cases, a naturally-occurring human trait. Most of us, it seems, are more than willing to stick out our chests and say, "Look at me; I did that!" But in our better moments, in the quiet moments when we search the depths of our own hearts, we know better. Whatever "it" is, God did that not us.

St. Augustine observed, "If you plan to build a tall house of virtues, you must first lay deep foundations of humility." Are you a believer who genuinely seeks to build your house of virtues on a strong foundation of humility? If so, you are wise and you are blessed. But if you've been laboring under the misconception that you're a "self-made" man or woman, it's time to face facts: your blessings come from God. And He deserves the credit.

We can never have more of true faith than we have of true humility.

Andrew Murray

Values for Life

Do you value humility above status? If so, God will smile upon your endeavors. But if you value status above humility, you're inviting God's displeasure. In short, humility pleases God; pride does not.

Timeless Wisdom for Godly Living

We are never stronger than the moment we admit we are weak.

Beth Moore

Jesus had a humble heart. If He abides in us,
pride will never dominate our lives.

Billy Graham

Humility is a thing which must be genuine;
the imitation of it is the nearest thing in the world to pride.

C. H. Spurgeon

God is against the proud,
but he gives grace to the humble.

1 Peter 5:5 NCV

God is attracted to weakness.
He can't resist those who humbly and honestly admit
how desperately they need him.

Jim Cymbala

Nothing sets a person so much out of the devil's reach as humility.

Jonathan Edwards

More Words from God's Word

If My people who are called by My name will humble themselves, and pray and seek My face, and turn from their wicked ways, then I will hear from heaven, and will forgive their sin and heal their land.

2 Chronicles 7:14 NKJV

This is the one I [God] esteem: he who is humble and contrite in spirit, and trembles at my word.

Isaiah 66:2 NIV

Humble yourselves in the sight of the Lord, and he shall lift you up.

James 4:10 KJV

He has showed you, O man, what is good. And what does the LORD *require of you? To act justly and to love mercy and to walk humbly with your God.*

Micah 6:8 NIV

My Values for Life

	Check Your Value		
	High	Med.	Low
I place a high priority on the need to remain humble before God . . .	___	___	___
I understand the importance of remaining humble in my dealings with others . . .	___	___	___
I genuinely seek to give God the honor that He deserves . . .	___	___	___

The Value of a Clear Conscience

So I strive always to keep my conscience clear before God and man.

Acts 24:16 NIV

It has been said that character is what we are when nobody is watching. How true. When we do things that we know aren't right, we try to hide them from our families and friends. But even then, God is watching.

Few things in life torment us more than a guilty conscience. And, few things in life provide more contentment than the knowledge that we are obeying God's commandments. A clear conscience is one of the rewards we earn when we obey God's Word and follow His will. When we follow God's will and accept His gift of salvation, our earthly rewards are never-ceasing, and our heavenly rewards are everlasting.

Billy Graham correctly observed, "Most of us follow our conscience as we follow a wheelbarrow. We push it in front of us in the direction we want to go." If that describes you, then here's a word of warning: both you and your wheelbarrow are headed for trouble.

Do you place a high value on the need to keep your conscience clear? If so, keep up the good work. But if you're tempted to do something that you'd rather the world not know about, remember this: You can sometimes keep secrets from other people, but you can never keep secrets from God. God knows what you think and what you do. And if you want to please Him, you must start with good intentions, a pure heart, and a clear conscience.

If you sincerely wish to honor your Father in heaven, follow His commandments. When you do, your character will take care of itself . . . and so will your conscience. Then, as you journey through life, you won't need to look over your shoulder to see who—besides God—is watching.

A good conscience is a continual feast.

Francis Bacon

Values for Life

Listening to that little voice . . . That quiet little voice inside your head will guide you down the right path if you listen carefully. Very often, your conscience will actually tell you what God wants you to do. So listen, learn, and behave accordingly.

Timeless Wisdom for Godly Living

To go against one's conscience is neither safe nor right.
Here I stand. I cannot do otherwise.

Martin Luther

Paul looked straight at the Sanhedrin and said, "My brothers, I have fulfilled my duty to God in all good conscience to this day."

Acts 23:1 NIV

The beginning of backsliding means your conscience does not answer to the truth.

Oswald Sanders

If I am walking along the street with a very disfiguring hole in the back of my dress, of which I am in ignorance, it is certainly a very great comfort to me to have a kind friend who will tell me of it. And similarly, it is indeed a comfort to know that there is always abiding with me a divine, all-seeing Comforter, who will reprove me for all my faults and will not let me go on in a fatal unconsciousness of them.

Hannah Whitall Smith

One's conscience can only be satisfied when God is satisfied.

C. H. *Spurgeon*

More Words from God's Word

Let us come near to God with a sincere heart and a sure faith, because we have been made free from a guilty conscience, and our bodies have been washed with pure water.

Hebrews 10:22 NCV

I will maintain my righteousness and never let go of it; my conscience will not reproach me as long as I live.

Job 27:6 NIV

Do not conform any longer to the pattern of this world, but be transformed by the renewing of your mind. Then you will be able to test and approve what God's will is—his good, pleasing and perfect will.

Romans 12:2 NIV

I tell the truth in Christ, I am not lying, my conscience also bearing me witness in the Holy Spirit . . . .

Romans 9:1 NKJV

My Values for Life

	Check Your Value		
	High	Med.	Low
I consider the value of a clear conscience to be . . .	___	___	___
I believe that it is important that I attune my thoughts to God's will for my life . . .	___	___	___
When I am about to make an important decision, I listen to my conscience *very* carefully . . .	___	___	___

The Power of Optimism

For God has not given us a spirit of fearfulness,
but one of power, love, and sound judgment.

2 Timothy 1:7 HCSB

Are you a hope-filled, enthusiastic Christian? You should be. After all, as a believer, you have every reason to be optimistic about your life here on earth and your eternal life in heaven. As English clergyman William Ralph Inge observed, "No Christian should be a pessimist, for Christianity is a system of radical optimism." Inge's words are most certainly true, but sometimes, you may find yourself pulled down by the inevitable concerns of everyday life. If you find yourself discouraged, exhausted, or both, then it's time to ask yourself this question: what's bothering you, and why?

If you're overly worried by the inevitable ups and downs of life, God wants to have a little chat with you. After all, God has made promises to you that He intends to keep. And if your life has been transformed by God's only begotten Son, then you, as a recipient of God's grace, have every reason to live courageously.

Are you willing to trust God's plans for your life? Hopefully, you will trust Him completely. After all, the words of the Psalmist make it clear: "The ways of God are without fault. The LORD's words are pure. He is a shield to those who trust him" (Psalm 18:30 NCV).

Woodroll Kroll noted, "If our minds are stayed upon God, His peace will rule the affairs entertained by our minds. If, on the other hand, we allow our minds to dwell on the cares of this world, God's peace will be far from our thoughts." These words should serve as a reminder that even when the challenges of the day seem daunting, God remains steadfast. And, so should you.

So make this promise to yourself and keep it—vow to be an expectant, faith-filled Christian. Think optimistically about your life, your profession, your family, your future, and your purpose for living. Trust your hopes not your fears. Take time to celebrate God's glorious creation. And then, when you've filled your heart with hope and gladness, share your optimism with others. They'll be better for it, and so will you.

The popular idea of faith is of a certain obstinate optimism:
the hope, tenaciously held in the face of trouble,
that the universe is fundamentally friendly and things may get better.

J. I. Packer

Values for Life

Be a realistic optimist: You should strive to think realistically about the future, but you should never confuse realism with pessimism. Your attitude toward the future will help create your future, so you might as well put the self-fulfilling prophecy to work for you by being both a realist *and* an optimist. And remember that life is far too short to be a pessimist.

Timeless Wisdom for Godly Living

Make the least of all that goes and the most of all that comes.
Don't regret what is past. Cherish what you have.
Look forward to all that is to come. And most important of all,
rely moment by moment on Jesus Christ.

Gigi Graham Tchividjian

I can do everything through him that gives me strength.

Philippians 4:13 NIV

The essence of optimism is that it takes no account of the present,
but it is a source of inspiration, of vitality, and of hope.
Where others have resigned, it enables a man to hold his head high,
to claim the future for himself, and not abandon it to his enemy.

Dietrich Bonhoeffer

The people whom I have seen succeed best in life have always
been cheerful and hopeful people who went about their business
with a smile on their faces.

Charles Kingsley

If our hearts have been attuned to God through an abiding faith in
Christ, the result will be joyous optimism and good cheer.

Billy Graham

More Words from God's Word

My cup runs over. Surely goodness and mercy shall follow me all the days of my life; and I will dwell in the house of the LORD Forever.

Psalm 23:5-6 NKJV

Finally, brethren, whatsoever things are true, whatsoever things are honest, whatsoever things are just, whatsoever things are pure, whatsoever things are lovely, whatsoever things are of good report; if there be any virtue, and if there be any praise, think on these things.

Philippians 4:8 KJV

But if we look forward to something we don't have yet, we must wait patiently and confidently.

Romans 8:25 NLT

My Values for Life

	Check Your Value		
	High	Med.	Low
Because my attitude helps shape my future, the importance that I place on maintaining a positive attitude is . . .	___	___	___
Because I believe that attitudes are contagious, I think it is helpful to associate with people who are optimistic and enthusiastic . . .	___	___	___
I believe that I can—and should—take steps to ensure that my attitude reflects my faith in God's promises . . .	___	___	___

Materialism 101: The Value of Stuff

Yes, a person is a fool to store up earthly wealth but not have a rich relationship with God.

Luke 12:21 NLT

In our demanding world, financial prosperity can be a good thing, but spiritual prosperity is profoundly more important. Certainly we all need the basic necessities of life, but once we meet those needs for our families and ourselves, the piling up of possessions creates more problems than it solves. Our real riches, of course, are not of this world. We are never *really* rich until we are rich in spirit. Yet we live in a society that leads us to believe otherwise. The media often glorifies material possessions above all else; God most certainly does not.

Martin Luther observed, "Many things I have tried to grasp and have lost. That which I have placed in God's hands I still have." His words apply to all of us. Our earthly riches are transitory; our spiritual riches, on the other hand, are everlasting.

How much value do you place on your material possessions? And while you're pondering that question, ask yourself this: Do you own your possessions or vice versa? If you don't like the answer you receive, make an ironclad promise to stop acquiring and start divesting.

Once you stop spending your hard-earned money on frivolous purchases, you'll be amazed at the things you can do without. You'll be pleasantly surprised at the sense of satisfaction that accompanies your newfound moderation. And you'll soon discover that when it comes to material possessions, less truly is more.

Do you find yourself wrapped up in the concerns of the material world? If so, it's time to reorder your priorities and reassess your values. And then, it's time to begin storing up riches that will endure throughout eternity—the spiritual kind.

As faithful stewards of what we have, ought we not to give earnest thought to our staggering surplus?

Elisabeth Elliot

Values for Life

Materialism Made Simple: The world wants you to believe that "money and stuff" can buy happiness. Don't believe it! Genuine happiness comes not from money but from the things that money *can't* buy—starting, of course, with your relationship to God and His only begotten Son.

Timeless Wisdom for Godly Living

If you want to be truly happy, you won't find it on an endless quest for more stuff. You'll find it in receiving God's generosity and the passing that generosity along.

Bill Hybels

It's sobering to contemplate how much time, effort, sacrifice, compromise, and attention we give to acquiring and increasing our supply of something that is totally insignificant in eternity.

Anne Graham Lotz

There is absolutely no evidence that complexity and materialism lead to happiness. On the contrary, there is plenty of evidence that simplicity and spirituality lead to joy, a blessedness that is better than happiness.

Dennis Swanberg

When we put people before possessions in our hearts, we are sowing seeds of enduring satisfaction.

Beverly LaHaye

Getting a little greedy? Pray without seizing.

Anonymous

For where your treasure is, there your heart will be also.

Luke 12:34 NKJV

More Words from God's Word

For what will it profit a man if he gains the whole world, and loses his own soul? Or what will a man give in exchange for his soul?

Mark 8:36-37 NKJV

He who trusts in his riches will fall, but the righteous will flourish . . . .

Proverbs 11:28 NKJV

No one can serve two masters.
The person will hate one master and love the other,
or will follow one master and refuse to follow the other.
You cannot serve both God and worldly riches.

Matthew 6:24 NCV

Keep your lives free from the love of money,
and be satisfied with what you have.

Hebrews 13:5 NCV

My Values for Life

	Check Your Value		
	High	Med.	Low
I don't expect material possessions to bring me lasting happiness . . .	___	___	___
I believe that my possessions are actually God's possessions, so I try to use them for His purposes . . .	___	___	___
My spending habits reflect the values that I hold most dear, so I try my best to be a faithful steward of my resources . . .	___	___	___

Sharing Your Testimony

All those who stand before others and say they believe in me,
I will say before my Father in heaven that they belong to me.

Matthew 10:32 NCV

Have you made the decision to allow Christ to reign over your heart? If so, you have an important story to tell: yours. Your personal testimony is profoundly important, but perhaps because of shyness (or because of the fear of being rebuffed), you've been hesitant to share your experiences. If so, you should start paying less attention to your own insecurities and more attention to the message that God wants you to share with the world.

In his second letter to Timothy, Paul shares a message to believers of every generation when he writes, "God has not given us a spirit of timidity" (1:7 NASB). Paul's meaning is clear: When sharing our testimonies, we must be courageous, forthright, and unashamed.

Corrie ten Boom observed, "There is nothing anybody else can do that can stop God from using us. We can turn *everything* into a testimony." Her words remind us that when we speak up for God, our actions may speak even more loudly than our words.

When we let other people know the details of our faith, we assume an important responsibility: the responsibility of making certain that our words are reinforced by our actions. When we share our testimonies, we must also be willing to serve as shining examples of righteousness—undeniable examples of the changes that Jesus makes in the lives of those who accept Him as their Savior.

Are you willing to follow in the footsteps of Jesus? If so, you must also be willing to talk about Him. And make no mistake—the time to express your belief in Him is now. You know how He has touched your own heart; help Him do the same for others.

To stand in an uncaring world and say,
"See, here is the Christ" is a daring act of courage.

Calvin Miller

Values for Life

Your story is important: D. L. Moody, the famed evangelist from Chicago, said, "Remember, a small light will do a great deal when it is in a very dark place. Put one little tallow candle in the middle of a large hall, and it will give a great deal of light." Make certain that your candle is always lit. Give your testimony, and trust God to do the rest.

Timeless Wisdom for Godly Living

Our Lord is searching for people who will make a difference. Christians dare not dissolve into the background or blend into the neutral scenery of the world.

Charles Swindoll

But when the Holy Spirit has come upon you, you will receive power and will tell people about me everywhere—in Jerusalem, throughout Judea, in Samaria, and to the ends of the earth.

Acts 1:8 NLT

One of the deepest pleas Christ made to His Father on the eve of the Crucifixion is that His followers would be one. "May they be brought to complete unity to let the world know that you sent me and have loved them even as you have loved me" (John 17:23). Unity unleashes such a powerful testimony that, through it, Christ said the world would know that God sent Him.

Beth Moore

How many people have you made homesick for God?

Oswald Chambers

More Words from God's Word

But the following night the Lord stood by him and said,
"Be of good cheer, Paul; for as you have testified for Me."

Acts 23:11 NKJV

Be wise in the way you act with people who are not believers,
making the most of every opportunity.

Colossians 4:5 NCV

You are the light of the world.

Matthew 5:14 NIV

We are therefore Christ's ambassadors,
as though God were making his appeal through us.
We implore you on Christ's behalf: Be reconciled to God.

2 Corinthians 5:20 NIV

My Values for Life

	Check Your Value		
	High	Med.	Low
The importance that I place on sharing my personal testimony . . .	___	___	___
The importance that I place on making certain that my actions are consistent with my words	___	___	___
I believe that every day presents another opportunity to share Christ's message with my family, with my friends, and with the world . . .	___	___	___

The Value of Your Daily Devotional

Stay clear of silly stories that get dressed up as religion. Exercise daily in God—no spiritual flabbiness, please!

1 Timothy 4:7 MSG

Each day has 1,440 minutes—do you value your relationship with God enough to spend a few of those minutes with Him? He deserves that much of your time *and more*—is He receiving it from you? Hopefully so. But if you find that you're simply "too busy" for a daily chat with your Father in heaven, it's time to take a long, hard look at your priorities and your values.

As you consider your plans for the day ahead, here's a tip: organize your life around this simple principle: "God first." When you place your Creator where He belongs—at the very center of your day and your life—the rest of your priorities will fall into place.

Each new day is a gift from God, and if you are wise, you will spend a few quiet moments each morning thanking the Giver. Daily life is woven together with the threads of habit, and no habit is more important to your spiritual health than the discipline of daily prayer and devotion to the Creator.

Warren Wiersbe writes, "Surrender your mind to the Lord at the beginning of each day." And that's sound advice. When you begin each day with your head bowed and your heart lifted, you are reminded of God's love, His protection, and His commandments.

Then, you can align your priorities for the coming day with the teachings and commandments that God has placed upon your heart.

So, if you've acquired the unfortunate habit of trying to "squeeze" God into the corners of your life, it's time to reshuffle the items on your to-do list by placing God first. God wants your undivided attention not the leftovers of your day. And if you haven't already done so, form the habit of spending quality time with your Father in heaven. He deserves it . . . and so, for that matter, do you.

Make a plan now to keep a daily appointment with God.
The enemy is going to tell you to set it aside,
but you must carve out the time.
If you're too busy to meet with the Lord, friend,
then you are simply too busy.

Charles Swindoll

Values for Life

How much time can you spare? Decide how much of your time God deserves, and then give it to Him. Don't organize your day so that God gets "what's left." Give Him what you honestly believe He deserves.

Timeless Wisdom for Godly Living

We all need to make time for God.
Even Jesus made time to be alone with the Father.

Kay Arthur

We must appropriate the tender mercy of God every day after conversion or problems quickly develop.
We need his grace daily in order to live a righteous life.

Jim Cymbala

What digestion is to the body, meditation is to the soul.

Warren Wiersbe

It is good to give thanks to the LORD,
to sing praises to the Most High.
It is good to proclaim your unfailing love in the morning,
your faithfulness in the evening.

Psalm 92:1-2 NLT

The moment you wake up each morning, all your wishes and hopes for the day rush at you like wild animals. And the first job each morning consists in shoving it all back; in listening to that other voice, taking that other point of view, letting that other, larger, stronger, quieter life coming flowing in.

C. S. *Lewis*

More Words from God's Word

Every morning he wakes me.
He teaches me to listen like a student.
The Lord God helps me learn . . . .

Isaiah 50:4-5 NCV

Be still, and know that I am God

Psalm 46:10 NKJV

In quietness and trust is your strength.

Isaiah 30:15 NASB

Let the words of my mouth and the meditation
of my heart be acceptable in Your sight,
O Lord, my strength and my Redeemer.

Psalm 19:14 NKJV

My Values for Life

Check Your Value		
High	Med.	Low

For me, the value of a daily devotional reading is . . . ___ ___ ___

The value of having a regular time and place where I can read, pray, and talk to God . . . ___ ___ ___

The value of quietly listening to the things that God places on my heart . . . ___ ___ ___

Character-building 101

The integrity of the upright guides them,
but the unfaithful are destroyed by their duplicity.

Proverbs 11:3 NIV

Catherine Marshall correctly observed, "The single most important element in any human relationship is honesty—with oneself, with God, and with others." Godly men and women agree. As believers in Christ, we must seek to live each day with discipline, honesty, and faith. When we do, at least two things happen: integrity becomes a habit, and God blesses us because of our obedience to Him. Living a life of integrity isn't always the *easiest* way, but it is always the *right* way . . . and God clearly intends that it should be *our* way, too.

Character isn't built overnight; it is built slowly over a lifetime. It is the sum of every right decision and every honest word. It is forged on the anvil of honorable work and polished by the twin virtues of honesty and fairness. Character is a precious thing—difficult to build and wonderful to behold.

Oswald Chambers, the author of the Christian classic *My Utmost for His Highest*, advised, "Never support an experience which does not have God as its source, and faith in God as its result." These words serve as a powerful reminder that as Christians we are called to walk with God and to obey His commandments. But, we live in a world that presents us with countless temptations to wander far from God's path. These temptations have the potential to destroy us, in part, because they cause us to be dishonest with ourselves and with others.

Dishonesty is a habit. Once we start bending the truth, we're likely to keep bending it. A far better strategy, of course, is to acquire the habit of being completely forthright with God, with other people, and with ourselves.

Honesty is also a habit, a habit that pays powerful dividends for those who place character above convenience. So, the next time you're tempted to bend the truth—or to break it—ask yourself this simple question: "What does God want me to do?" Then listen carefully to your conscience. When you do, your actions will be honorable, and your character will take care of itself.

Every secret act of character, conviction, and courage has been observed in living color by our omniscient God.

Bill Hybels

Values for Life

One of your greatest possessions is integrity . . . don't lose it. Billy Graham was right when he said: "Integrity is the glue that holds our way of life together. We must constantly strive to keep our integrity intact. When wealth is lost, nothing is lost; when health is lost, something is lost; when character is lost, all is lost."

Timeless Wisdom for Godly Living

Your true character is something that no one can injure but yourself.

C. H. Spurgeon

If I take care of my character, my reputation will take care of itself.

D. L. Moody

It is the thoughts and intents of the heart that shape a person's life.

John Eldredge

In everything set them an example by doing what is good. In your teaching show integrity, seriousness and soundness of speech that cannot be condemned, so that those who oppose you may be ashamed because they have nothing bad to say about us.

Titus 2:7 NIV

Sow an act and you reap a habit.
Sow a habit and you reap a character.
Sow a character and you reap a destiny.

Anonymous

Image is what people think we are; integrity is what we really are.

John Maxwell

More Words from God's Word

A good name is more desirable than great riches;
to be esteemed is better than silver or gold.

Proverbs 22:1 NIV

Blessed is the man who does not walk in the counsel of the wicked or stand in the way of sinners or sit in the seat of mockers. But his delight is in the law of the LORD, *and on his law he meditates day and night. He is like a tree planted by streams of water, which yields its fruit in season and whose leaf does not wither. Whatever he does prospers.*

Psalm 1:1-3 NIV

We also have joy with our troubles, because we know that these troubles produce patience. And patience produces character, and character produces hope.

Romans 5:3-4 NCV

My Values for Life

	Check Your Value		
	High	Med.	Low
The value that I place upon living a life of integrity is . . .	___	___	___
Removing myself from situations that might compromise my integrity has a value that is . . .	___	___	___
I believe that I should hold myself accountable for the things that I say and do . . .	___	___	___

The Value of Kindness

And be kind and compassionate to one another,
forgiving one another, just as God also forgave you in Christ.
Ephesians 4:3 HCSB

John Wesley's advice was straightforward: "Do all the good you can. By all the means you can. In all the ways you can. In all the places you can. At all the times you can. To all the people you can. As long as you can." One way to do all the good we can is to spread kindness wherever we go.

Sometimes, when we feel happy or generous, we find it easy to be kind. Other times, when we are discouraged or tired, we can scarcely summon the energy to utter a single kind word. But, God's commandment is clear: He intends that we make the conscious choice to treat others with kindness and respect, no matter our circumstances, no matter our emotions.

For Christians, kindness is not an option; it is a commandment. In the Gospel of Matthew, Jesus declares, "In everything, therefore, treat people the same way you want them to treat you, for this is the Law and the Prophets" (Matthew 7:12 NASB). Jesus did not say, "In some things, treat people as you wish to be treated." And, He did not say, "From time to time, treat others with kindness." Christ said that we should treat others as we wish to be treated "in everything." This, of course, is a difficult task, but as Christians, we are commanded to do our best.

Today, as you consider all the things that Christ has done in your life, honor Him by being a little kinder than necessary. Honor Him by slowing down long enough to offer encouragement to someone who needs it. Honor Him by picking up the phone and calling a distant friend . . . for no reason other than to say, "I'm thinking of you." Honor Christ with your good words and your good deeds. Jesus expects no less, and He deserves no less.

The mark of a Christian is that he will walk the second mile and turn the other cheek. A wise man or woman gives the extra effort, all for the glory of the Lord Jesus Christ.

John Maxwell

Values for Life

You can't just talk about it: In order to be a kind person, you must not only think kind thoughts; you must also do kind things. So get busy! The best day to become a more generous person is *this* day!

Timeless Wisdom for Godly Living

When you extend hospitality to others,
you're not trying to impress people,
you're trying to reflect God to them.

Max Lucado

Kindness in this world will do much to help others,
not only to come into the light, but also to grow in grace day by day.

Fanny Crosby

Here is a simple, rule-of-thumb for behavior:
Ask yourself what you want people to do for you,
then grab the initiative and do it for them.
Add up God's Law and Prophets and this is what you get.

Matthew 7:12 MSG

Be so preoccupied with good will that you haven't room for ill will.

E. Stanley Jones

Be such a man, and live such a life, that if every man were such as you,
and every life a life like yours, this earth would be God's Paradise.

Phillips Brooks

When you launch an act of kindness out into the crosswinds of life,
it will blow kindness back to you.

Dennis Swanberg

More Words from God's Word

*Each of you should look not only to your own interests,
but also to the interest of others.*

Philippians 2:4 NIV

*We must not become tired of doing good. We will receive our harvest
of eternal life at the right time if we do not give up.*

Galatians 6:9 NCV

A kind man benefits himself, but a cruel man brings trouble on himself.

Proverbs 11:17 NIV

*Be kindly affectionate to one another with brotherly love,
in honor giving preference to one another; not lagging in diligence,
fervent in spirit, serving the Lord; rejoicing in hope, patient in tribulation,
continuing steadfastly in prayer.*

Romans 12:10-12 NKJV

My Values for Life

	Check Your Value		
	High	Med.	Low
As a Christian, I feel that it is my obligation to be kind to others . . .	___	___	___
In all my decisions I seek to apply the Golden Rule.	___	___	___
When I extend the hand of kindness to others, I feel that it is important for me to avoid public acclaim . . .	___	___	___

Tackling Tough Times

In this world you will have trouble.
But take heart! I have overcome the world.

John 16:33 NIV

As life unfolds, all of us encounter occasional setbacks: Those periodic visits from Old Man Trouble are simply a fact of life, and none of us are exempt. When tough times arrive, we may be forced to rearrange our plans, but we must never rearrange our values.

The fact that we encounter adversity is not nearly so important as the way we choose to deal with it. When tough times arrive, we have a clear choice: we can begin the difficult work of tackling our troubles . . . or not. When we summon the courage to look Old Man Trouble squarely in the eye, he usually blinks. But, if we refuse to address our problems, even the smallest annoyances have a way of growing into king-sized catastrophes.

Psalm 145 promises, "The LORD is near to all who call on him, to all who call on him in truth. He fulfills the desires of those who fear him; he hears their cry and saves them" (vv. 18-20 NIV). And the words of Jesus offer us comfort: "I tell you the truth, you will weep and mourn while the world rejoices. You will grieve, but your grief will turn to joy" (John 16:20 NIV).

As believers, we know that God loves us and that He will protect us. In times of hardship, He will comfort us; in times of sorrow, He will dry our tears. When we are troubled or weak or sorrowful, God is always with us. We must build our lives on the rock that cannot be shaken: we must trust in God. And then, we must get on with the hard work of tackling our problems . . . because if we don't, who will? Or should?

You cannot persevere unless there is a trial in your life.
There can be no victories without battles; there can be
no peaks without valleys. If you want the blessing, you must be
prepared to carry the burden and fight the battle.
God has to balance privileges with responsibilities,
blessings with burdens, or else you and
I will become spoiled, pampered children.

Warren Wiersbe

Values for Life

Tough Times 101: Sometimes, when we encounter tough times, we find ourselves "starting over." From scratch. As believers we can find comfort in the knowledge that wherever we find ourselves, whether on the mountaintops of life or in the deepest valleys of despair, God is there with us. And just as importantly, we never have to "start over" with Him, because He never left us!

Timeless Wisdom for Godly Living

It's time we stopped groaning over our adversaries and started glorying in our allies. The battle is the Lord's. The victory is already won. Our Waterloo is behind us.

Vance Havner

If you learn from a defeat, you have not really lost.

Zig Ziglar

We are hard pressed on every side, yet not crushed; we are perplexed, but not in despair.

2 Corinthians 4:8 NKJV

"But he knows the way that I take; when he has tested me, I will come forth as gold" (Job 23:10 NIV). We will all "come forth as gold" if we understand that God is sovereign and knows what is best, even when we cannot understand what is happening at the time.

Shirley Dobson

God helps those who help themselves, but there are times when we are quite incapable of helping ourselves. That's when God stoops down and gathers us in His arms like a mother lifts a sick child, and does for us what we cannot do for ourselves.

Ruth Bell Graham

More Words from God's Word

I have heard your prayer, I have seen your tears; surely I will heal you.

2 Kings 20:5 NKJV

In my distress I called to the LORD; I called out to my God.
From his temple he heard my voice; my cry came to his ears.

2 Samuel 22:7 NIV

A time to weep, and a time to laugh; a time to mourn,
and a time to dance . . . .

Ecclesiastes 3:4 KJV

Consider it pure joy, my brothers, whenever you face trials of many kinds, because you know that the testing of your faith develops perseverance. Perseverance must finish its work so that you may be mature and complete, not lacking anything.

James 1:2-4 NIV

My Values for Life

	Check Your Value		
	High	Med.	Low
In dealing with difficult situations, I view God as my comfort and my strength . . .	___	___	___
I believe that difficult times can also be times of intense personal growth . . .	___	___	___
I understand the importance of comforting others who find themselves in difficult circumstances . . .	___	___	___

An Attitude That Is Pleasing to God

Keep your eyes focused on what is right,
and look straight ahead to what is good.

Proverbs 4:25 NCV

The Christian life is a cause for celebration, but sometimes we don't feel much like celebrating. In fact, when the weight of the world seems to bear down upon our shoulders, celebration may be the last thing on our minds . . . but it shouldn't be. As God's children, we are all blessed beyond measure on good days and bad. This day is a non-renewable resource—once it's gone, it's gone forever. We should give thanks for this day while using it for the glory of God.

What's your attitude today? Are you fearful, angry, bored, or worried? Are you pessimistic, perplexed, pained, and perturbed? Are you moping around with a frown on your face that's almost as big as the one in your heart? If so, God wants to have a little talk with you.

God created you in His own image, and He wants you to experience joy, contentment, peace, and abundance. But, God will not force you to experience these things; you must claim them for yourself.

God has given you free will, including the ability to influence the direction and the tone of your thoughts. And, here's how God wants you to direct those thoughts:

> *Finally brothers, whatever is true, whatever is honorable, whatever is just, whatever is pure, whatever is lovely, whatever is commendable—if there is any moral excellence and if there is any praise—dwell on these things" (Philippians 4:8* HCSB*).*

The quality of your attitude will help determine the quality of your life, so you must guard your thoughts accordingly. If you make up your mind to approach life with a healthy mixture of realism and optimism, you'll be rewarded. But, if you allow yourself to fall into the unfortunate habit of negative thinking, you will doom yourself to unhappiness or mediocrity or worse.

So, the next time you find yourself dwelling upon the negative aspects of your life, refocus your attention on things positive. The next time you find yourself falling prey to the blight of pessimism, stop yourself and turn your thoughts around. The next time you're tempted to waste valuable time gossiping or complaining, resist those temptations with all your might.

And remember: You'll never whine your way to the top . . . so don't waste your breath.

Do you feel the world is treating you well? If your attitude toward the world is excellent, you will receive excellent results. If you feel so-so about the world, your response from that world will be average. If you feel badly about your world, you will seem to have only negative feedback from life.

John Maxwell

Values for Life

Focus on possibilities not stumbling blocks: Of course you will encounter occasional disappointments, and, from time to time, you will encounter failure. But, don't invest large amounts of energy focusing on past misfortunes. Instead, look to the future with optimism and hope.

Timeless Wisdom for Godly Living

Your attitude, not your aptitude, will determine your altitude.

Zig Ziglar

Your attitude should be the same as that of Christ Jesus: Who, being in very nature God, did not consider equality with God something to be grasped, but made himself nothing, taking the very nature of a servant, being made in human likeness. And being found in appearance as a man, he humbled himself and became obedient to death—even death on a cross!

Philippians 2:5-8 NIV

The purity of motive determines the quality of action.

Oswald Chambers

I could go through this day oblivious to the miracles all around me, or I could tune in and "enjoy."

Gloria Gaither

Some people complain that God put thorns on roses, while others praise Him for putting roses on thorns.

Anonymous

More Words from God's Word

*A miserable heart means a miserable life;
a cheerful heart fills the day with a song.*

Proverbs 15:15 MSG

Therefore, since Christ suffered in his body, arm yourselves also with the same attitude, because he who has suffered in his body is done with sin. As a result, he does not live the rest of his earthly life for evil human desires, but rather for the will of God.

1 Peter 4:1-2 NIV

You were taught, with regard to your former way of life, to put off your old self, which is being corrupted by its deceitful desires; to be made new in the attitude of your minds; and to put on the new self, created to be like God in true righteousness and holiness.

Ephesians 4:22-24 NIV

My Values for Life

	Check Your Value		
	High	Med.	Low
For me, the value that I place on maintaining a positive attitude is . . .	___	___	___
The importance of directing my thoughts and to my blessings rather than to my challenges . . .	___	___	___
The importance of surrounding myself with people who are positive, enthusiastic, and encouraging . . .	___	___	___

The Value (and the Power) of Prayer

When a believing person prays, great things happen.

James 5:16 NCV

Does prayer play an important role in your life? Is prayer an integral part of your daily routine, or is it a hit-or-miss activity? Do you "pray without ceasing," or is your prayer life an afterthought? If you genuinely wish to receive that abundance that Christ promises in John 10:10, then you must pray constantly . . . and you must *never* underestimate the power of prayer.

As you contemplate the quality of your prayer life, here are a few things to consider:

1. God hears our prayers and answers them (Jeremiah 29:11-12).

2. God promises that the prayers of righteous men and women can accomplish great things (James 5:16).

3. God invites us to be still and to feel His presence (Psalm 46:10).

So pray. Start praying in the early morning and keep praying until you fall off to sleep at night. Pray about matters great and small; and be watchful for the answers that God most assuredly sends your way.

Daily prayer and meditation are a matter of will and habit.

When you organize your day to include quiet moments with God, you'll soon discover that no time is more precious than the silent moments you spend with Him.

The quality of your spiritual life will be in direct proportion to the quality of your prayer life. So do yourself a favor: instead of turning things over in your mind, turn them over to God in prayer. Instead of worrying about your next decision, ask God to lead the way. Don't limit your prayers to meals or to bedtime. Pray constantly because God is listening—and He wants to hear from you. And without question, you need to hear from Him.

You don't need fancy words or religious phrases.
Just tell God the way it really is.

Jim Cymbala

Values for Life

Prayer strengthens our relationship with God . . . Beth Moore writes, "Prayer keeps us in constant communion with God, which is the goal of our entire believing lives." It's up to each of us to live—and pray—accordingly.

Timeless Wisdom for Godly Living

We must understand that the only ones who prepare themselves for prayer adequately are those who are so impressed with God's majesty that they can be free from all earthly worries and afflictions.

John Calvin

For the eyes of the Lord are over the righteous,
and his ears are open unto their prayers:
but the face of the Lord is against them that do evil.

1 Peter 3:12 KJV

Are you weak? Weary? Confused? Troubled? Pressured?
How is your relationship with God? Is it held in its place of priority?
I believe the greater the pressure,
the greater your need for time alone with Him.

Kay Arthur

When you ask God to do something, don't ask timidly;
put your whole heart into it.

Marie T. Freeman

As it is the business of tailors to make clothes and
cobblers to make shoes, so it is the business of Christians to pray.

Martin Luther

More Words from God's Word

Rejoice always! Pray constantly. Give thanks in everything, for this is God's will for you in Christ Jesus.

1 Thessalonians 5:16-18 HCSB

And it will come about that whoever calls on the name of the LORD will be delivered.

Joel 2:32 NASB

Whatever you ask for in prayer, believe that you have received it, and it will be yours.

Mark 11:24 NIV

Be anxious for nothing, but in everything by prayer and supplication with thanksgiving let your requests be made known to God.

Philippians 4:6 NASB

My Values for Life

Statement	Check Your Value: High	Med.	Low
The value that I place upon prayer is . . .	___	___	___
For me, the importance of praising God is . . .	___	___	___
Even when prayer does not change my circumstances, I feel that prayer is essential because it changes me . . .	___	___	___

Following in His Footsteps

Then Jesus said to his disciples, "If anyone would come after me, he must deny himself and take up his cross and follow me. For whoever wants to save his life will lose it, but whoever loses his life for me will find it."

Matthew 16:24-25 NIV

When Jesus addressed His disciples, He warned that each one must "take up his cross and follow me." The disciples must have known exactly what the Master meant. In Jesus' day, prisoners were forced to carry their own crosses to the location where they would be put to death. Thus, Christ's message was clear: in order to follow Him, Christ's disciples must deny themselves and, instead, trust Him completely. Nothing has changed since then.

If we are to be disciples of Christ, we must trust Him and place Him at the very center of our beings. Jesus never comes "next." He is always first. The paradox, of course, is that only by sacrificing ourselves to Him do we gain salvation for ourselves.

The 19th-century writer Hannah Whitall Smith observed, "The crucial question for each of us is this: What do you think of Jesus, and do you yet have a personal acquaintance with Him?" Indeed, the answer to that question will determine the quality, the course, and the direction of your life today and for all eternity.

Jesus has called upon believers of every generation (and that includes you) to walk with Him. Jesus promises that when you follow in His footsteps, He will teach you how to live freely and lightly (Matthew 11:28-30). And when Jesus makes a promise, you can depend upon it.

Are you worried or anxious? Be confident in the power of Christ. He will never desert you. Are you discouraged? Be courageous and call upon your Savior. He will protect you and use you according to His purposes. Do you seek to be a worthy disciple of the One from Galilee? Then pick up His cross today and every day of your life. When you do, He will bless you now . . . *and* forever.

Teach a man a rule and you help him solve a problem; teach a man to walk with God and you help him solve the rest of his life.

John Eldredge

Values for Life

If you want to be a disciple of Christ . . . follow in His footsteps, obey His commandments, and share His never-ending love.

Timeless Wisdom for Godly Living

Think of this—we may live together with Him here and now,
a daily walking with Him who loved us and gave Himself for us.

Elisabeth Elliot

Our responsibility is to feed from Him, to stay close to Him,
to follow Him—because sheep easily go astray—
so that we eternally experience the protection and
companionship of our Great Shepherd the Lord Jesus Christ.

Franklin Graham

*As you therefore have received Christ Jesus the Lord,
so walk with him.*

Colossians 2:6 NASB

Christ is like a river that is continually flowing.
There are always fresh supplies of water coming from
the fountain-head, so that a man may live by it and be supplied with
water all his life. So Christ is an ever-flowing fountain;
he is continually supplying his people, and the fountain is not spent.
They who live upon Christ may have fresh supplies from him for
all eternity; they may have an increase of blessedness that is new,
and new still, and which never will come to an end.

Jonathan Edwards

More Words from God's Word

I am the light of the world. Whoever follows me will never walk in darkness, but will have the light of life.

John 8:12 NIV

Are you tired? Worn out? Burned out on religion? Come to me. Get away with me and you'll recover your life. I'll show you how to take a real rest. Walk with me and work with me . . . watch how I do it. Learn the unforced rhythms of grace. I won't lay anything heavy or ill-fitting on you. Keep company with me and you'll learn to live freely and lightly.

Matthew 11:28-30 MSG

And what does the LORD require of you?
To act justly and to love mercy and to walk humbly with your God.

Micah 6:8 NIV

Whoever serves me must follow me. Then my servant will be with me everywhere I am. My Father will honor anyone who serves me.

John 12:26 NCV

My Values for Life

	Check Your Value		
	High	Med.	Low
For me, the importance of following Jesus is . . .	___	___	___
For me, discipleship means obedience . . .	___	___	___
For me, showing others I follow Christ is . . .	___	___	___

The Power of Perseverance

Even though good people may be bothered by trouble seven times, they are never defeated.

Proverbs 24:16 NCV

As you continue to seek God's purpose for your life, you will undoubtedly experience your fair share of disappointments, detours, false starts, and failures. When you do, don't become discouraged: God's not finished with you yet.

The old saying is as true today as it was when it was first spoken: "Life is a marathon, not a sprint." That's why wise travelers (like you) select a traveling companion who never tires and never falters. That partner, of course, is your Heavenly Father.

The next time you find your courage tested to the limit, remember that God is as near as your next breath, and remember that He offers strength and comfort to His children. He is your shield and your strength; He is your protector and your deliverer. Call upon Him in your hour of need and then be comforted. Whatever your challenge, whatever your trouble, God can help you persevere. And that's precisely what He'll do *if* you ask Him.

Perhaps you are in a hurry for God to help you resolve your difficulties. Perhaps you're anxious to earn the rewards that you feel you've already earned from life. Perhaps you're drumming your fingers, impatiently waiting for God to act. If so, be forewarned: God operates on His own timetable not yours. Sometimes, God may answer your prayers with silence, and when He does, you must patiently persevere. In times of trouble, you must remain steadfast and trust in the merciful goodness of your Heavenly Father. Whatever your problem, He can handle it. Your job is to keep persevering until He does.

By perseverance the snail reached the ark.

C. H. Spurgeon

Values for Life

Feeling tired, troubled, and discouraged? Maybe you're not getting enough sleep. Do you get a full eight hours of sleep each night? You should. To be sufficiently strong tomorrow, you need sufficient sleep tonight.

Timeless Wisdom for Godly Living

Battles are won in the trenches, in the grit and grime of courageous determination; they are won day by day in the arena of life.

Charles Swindoll

Failure is one of life's most powerful teachers.
How we handle our failures determines whether
we're going to simply "get by" in life or "press on."

Beth Moore

All rising to a great place is by a winding stair.

Francis Bacon

Don't look for shortcuts to God. The market is flooded with surefire, easygoing formulas for a successful life that can be practiced in your spare time. Don't fall for that stuff, even though crowds of people do. The way to life—to God!—is vigorous and requires total attention.

Matthew 7:13-14 MSG

Keep adding, keep walking, keep advancing; do not stop, do not turn back, do not turn from the straight road.

St. Augustine

More Words from God's Word

Indeed we count them blessed who endure.

James 5:11 NKJV

Blessed is the man who perseveres under trial,
because when he has stood the test, he will receive the crown of life
that God has promised to those who love him.

James 1:12 NIV

Let us not lose heart in doing good, for in due time we shall reap
if we do not grow weary. So then, while we have opportunity,
let us do good to all men, and especially to those who are
of the household of the faith.

Galatians 6:9-10 NASB

I have fought a good fight, I have finished my course,
I have kept the faith.

2 Timothy 4:7 KJV

My Values for Life

	Check Your Value		
	High	Med.	Low
The value that I place upon perseverance is . . .	___	___	___
When I am discouraged, I ask God to help me be strong . . .	___	___	___
For me, it is helpful to associate with people who encourage me to be courageous, optimistic, and energetic . . .	___	___	___

The Right Thing to Do

But prove yourselves doers of the word,
and not merely hearers.

James 1:22 NASB

If you're like most people, you seek the admiration of your neighbors, your coworkers, and your family members. But the eagerness to please others should never overshadow your eagerness to please God. If you seek to fulfill the purposes that God has in store for you, then you must be a "doer of the word." And how can you do so? By putting God first.

The words of Matthew 6:33 make it clear: "But seek first the kingdom of God and His righteousness, and all these things will be provided for you" (HCSB). God has given you a priceless guidebook, an indispensable tool for "seeking His kingdom." That tool, of course, is the Holy Bible. It contains thorough instructions which, if followed, lead to fulfillment, righteousness, and salvation.

But for those who would ignore God's Word, Martin Luther issued this stern warning: "You may as well quit reading and hearing the Word of God and give it to the devil if you do not desire to live according to it." Luther understood that obedience leads to abundance just as surely as disobedience leads to disaster; you should understand it, too.

Each new day presents countless opportunities to put God in first place . . . or not. When you honor Him by living according to His commandments, you earn the abundance and peace that He promises.

But, if you ignore God's teachings, you will inevitably bring needless suffering upon yourself and your family.

Would you like a time-tested formula for successful living? Here it is: Don't just listen to God's Word; live by it. Does this sound too simple? Perhaps it is simple, but it is also the only way to reap the marvelous riches that God has in store for you.

The best evidence of our having the truth is
our walking in the truth.

Matthew Henry

Values for Life

Obey God or face the consequences: God rewards obedience and punishes disobedience. It's not enough to understand God's rules; you must also live by them . . . or else.

Timeless Wisdom for Godly Living

Resolved: never to do anything which I should be afraid to do if it were the last hour of my life.

Jonathan Edwards

Righteousness not only defines God, but God defines righteousness.

Bill Hybels

By this we know that we have come to know Him, if we keep His commandments.

1 John 2:3 NASB

Christians are the citizens of heaven, and while we are on earth, we ought to behave like heaven's citizens.

Warren Wiersbe

What you do reveals what you believe about God, regardless of what you say. When God reveals what He has purposed to do, you face a crisis—a decision time. God and the world can tell from your response what you really believe about God.

Henry Blackaby

If we have the true love of God in our hearts, we will show it in our lives. We will not have to go up and down the earth proclaiming it. We will show it in everything we say or do.

D. L. Moody

More Words from God's Word

But now you must be holy in everything you do, just as God—who chose you to be his children—is holy. For he himself has said, "You must be holy because I am holy."

1 Peter 1:15-16 NLT

Walk in a manner worthy of the God who calls you into His own kingdom and glory.

1 Thessalonians 2:12 NASB

Discipline yourself for the purpose of godliness.

1 Timothy 4:7 NASB

Applying all diligence, in your faith supply moral excellence.

2 Peter 1:5 NASB

The LORD has sought out for Himself a man after His own heart.

1 Samuel 13:14 NASB

My Values for Life

	Check Your Value		
	High	Med.	Low
I believe that my values are reflected by my actions . . .	___	___	___
I believe that when I am obedient to God, He blesses my undertakings . . .	___	___	___
When I am a "doer of the word," I feel better about myself . . .	___	___	___

Always Here

The eyes of the LORD are in every place, keeping watch . . . .

Proverbs 15:3 NKJV

In the quiet early morning, as the sun's first rays stream over the horizon, we may sense the presence of God. But as the day wears on and the demands of everyday life bear down upon us, we may become so wrapped up in earthly concerns that we forget to praise the Creator.

God is everywhere we have ever been and everywhere we will ever be. When we turn to Him often, we are blessed by His presence. But, if we ignore God's presence or rebel against it altogether, the world in which we live soon becomes a spiritual wasteland.

Since God is everywhere, we are free to sense His presence whenever we take the time to quiet our souls and turn our prayers to Him. But sometimes, amid the incessant demands of everyday life, we turn our thoughts far from God; when we do, we suffer.

Do you set aside quiet moments each day to offer praise to your Creator? You should. During these moments of stillness, you can sense the infinite love and power of our Lord. The familiar words of Psalm 46:10 remind us to "Be still, and know that I am God" (KJV). When we do so, we encounter the awesome presence of our loving Heavenly Father.

Are you tired, discouraged, or fearful? Be comforted because God is with you. Are you confused? Listen to the quiet voice of your Heavenly Father. Are you bitter? Talk with God and seek His guidance. Are you celebrating a great victory? Thank God and praise Him. He is the Giver of all things good. In whatever condition you find yourself—whether you are happy or sad, victorious or vanquished, troubled or triumphant—celebrate God's presence. And be comforted in the knowledge that God is not just near. He is here.

If you want to hear God's voice clearly and you are uncertain, then remain in His presence until He changes that uncertainty. Often, much can happen during this waiting for the Lord. Sometimes, he changes pride into humility, doubt into faith and peace.

Corrie ten Boom

Values for Life

Having trouble hearing God? If so, slow yourself down, tune out the distractions, and listen carefully. God has important things to say; your task is to be still and listen.

Timeless Wisdom for Godly Living

There is a basic urge: the longing for unity.
You desire a reunion with God—with God your Father.

E. Stanley Jones

God walks with us. He scoops us up in His arms or simply sits with us in silent strength until we cannot avoid the awesome recognition that yes, even now, He is here.

Gloria Gaither

It's a crazy world and life speeds by at a blur, yet God is right in the middle of the craziness. And anywhere, at anytime, we may turn to Him, hear His voice, feel His hand, and catch the fragrance of heaven.

Joni Eareckson Tada

The next time you hear a baby laugh or see an ocean wave, take note. Pause and listen as his Majesty whispers ever so gently, "I'm here."

Max Lucado

Get yourself into the presence of the loving Father. Just place yourself before Him, and look up into His face; think of His love, His wonderful, tender, pitying love.

Andrew Murray

Be still, and know that I am God . . . .

Psalm 46:10 KJV

More Words from God's Word

The LORD Almighty is here among us; the God of Israel is our fortress. Come see the glorious works of the LORD . . . .

Psalm 46:7-8 NLT

Surely goodness and mercy shall follow me all the days of my life: and I will dwell in the house of the LORD for ever.

Psalm 23:6 KJV

Let your gentleness be evident to all. The Lord is near.

Philippians 4:5 NIV

Do not be afraid or discouraged.
For the LORD your God is with you wherever you go.

Joshua 1:9 NLT

My Values for Life

	Check Your Value		
	High	Med.	Low
The value that I place upon quiet communication with God . . .	___	___	___
The importance of having a regular time of prayer and reflection . . .	___	___	___
Because I am comforted by God's presence, I seek Him often . . .	___	___	___

The Power of the Words We Speak

Watch the way you talk. Let nothing foul or dirty come out of your mouth. Say only what helps, each word a gift.

Ephesians 4:29 MSG

How much value do you place on the words you speak? Hopefully, you understand that your words have great power . . . because they most certainly do. If your words are encouraging, you can lift others up; if your words are hurtful, you can hold others back.

The Bible makes it clear that "Reckless words pierce like a sword, but the tongue of the wise brings healing" (Proverbs 12:18 NIV). So, if you hope to solve problems instead of starting them, you must measure your words carefully. But sometimes, you'll be tempted to speak first and think second (with decidedly mixed results).

When you're frustrated or tired, you may say things that would be better left unspoken. Whenever you lash out in anger, you forgo the wonderful opportunity to consider your thoughts before you give voice to them. When you speak impulsively, you may, quite unintentionally, injure others.

A far better strategy, of course, is to do the more difficult thing: to think first and to speak next. When you do so, you give yourself ample time to compose your thoughts and to consult our Creator (but not necessarily in that order!).

The Bible warns that you will be judged by the words you speak (Matthew 12:36-37). And, Ephesians 4:29 instructs you to make "each word a gift" (MSG). These passages make it clear that God cares very much about the things you say *and* the way you say them. And if God cares that much, so should you.

Do you seek to be a source of encouragement to others? Are you a beacon of hope to your friends and family? And, do you seek to be a worthy ambassador for Christ? If so, you must speak words that are worthy of your Savior. So avoid angry outbursts. Refrain from impulsive outpourings. Terminate tantrums. Instead, speak words of encouragement and hope to a world that desperately needs both.

Words. Do you fully understand their power?
Can any of us really grasp the mighty force behind the things we say?
Do we stop and think before we speak,
considering the potency of the words we utter?

Joni Eareckson Tada

Values for Life

When in doubt, use the Golden Rule to help you decide what to say: If you wouldn't like for somebody to say it about you, don't say it about them!

Timeless Wisdom for Godly Living

A little kindly advice is better than a great deal of scolding.

Fanny Crosby

For out of the overflow of the heart the mouth speaks.

Matthew 12:34 NIV

When you talk, choose the very same words that you would use if Jesus were looking over your shoulder. Because He is.

Marie T. Freeman

Fill the heart with the love of Christ so that only truth and purity can come out of the mouth.

Warren Wiersbe

The battle of the tongue is won not in the mouth, but in the heart.

Annie Chapman

Perhaps we have been guilty of speaking against someone and have not realized how it may have hurt them. Then when someone speaks against us, we suddenly realize how deeply such words hurt, and we become sensitive to what we have done.

Theodore Epp

More Words from God's Word

Careless words stab like a sword, but wise words bring healing.

Proverbs 12:18 NCV

May the words of my mouth and the meditation of my heart be pleasing in your sight, O LORD, my Rock and my Redeemer.

Psalm 19:14 NIV

If you confess with your mouth, "Jesus is Lord," and believe in your heart that God raised him from the dead, you will be saved. For it is with your heart that you believe and are justified, and it is with your mouth that you confess and are saved.

Romans 10:9-10 NIV

Kind words are like honey—sweet to the soul and healthy for the body.

Proverbs 16:24 NLT

My Values for Life

	Check Your Value		
	High	Med.	Low
The value that I place on speaking words that are pleasing to God . . .	___	___	___
The importance of my willingness to encourage other people . . .	___	___	___
The value of associating with godly people who encourage me . . .	___	___	___

Enthusiasm for Today's Tasks

Whatever you do, do your work heartily,
as for the Lord rather than for men.

Colossians 3:23 NASB

Have you acquired the habit of doing first things first, or are you one of those people who put off important work until the last minute? The answer to this simple question will help determine how well you do your work and how much fun you have doing it.

God's Word teaches the value of hard work. In his second letter to the Thessalonians, Paul warns, ". . . if any would not work, neither should he eat" (3:10 KJV). And the Book of Proverbs proclaims, "One who is slack in his work is brother to one who destroys" (18:9 NIV). In short, God has created a world in which diligence is rewarded and laziness is not. So, whatever it is that you choose to do, do it with commitment, excitement, and vigor. And remember this: Hard work is not simply a proven way to get ahead; it's also part of God's plan for you.

Norman Vincent Peale said, "Think enthusiastically about everything, especially your work." If you're wise, you'll take that advice. When you do, you'll soon discover that the old saying is true: attitude determines altitude.

You have countless opportunities to accomplish great things for your God, for your family, and for yourself—but you should not expect the work to be easy. So pray as if everything depended upon God, but work as if everything depended upon you. When you do, you should expect very big payoffs. Why? Because when you and God become partners in your work, amazing things are bound to happen.

The world does not consider labor a blessing;
therefore it flees and hates it, but the pious who fear the Lord
labor with a ready and cheerful heart, for they know God's command,
and they acknowledge His calling.

Martin Luther

Values for Life

Have faith and get busy: Here's a time-tested formula for success: have faith in God and do the work. It has been said that there are no shortcuts to anyplace worth going. God did not create us for lives of mediocrity; He created us for far greater things. Earning great things usually requires work and lots of it, which is perfectly fine with God. After all, He knows that we're up to the task, and He has big plans for us. Very big plans . . .

Timeless Wisdom for Godly Living

Dear Lord, let us pray for our daily bread, but let us not be afraid to hunt for our corn-pone with sweat running down the hoe handle.

Sam Jones

Get absolutely enthralled with something.
Throw yourself into it with abandon.
Get out of yourself. Be somebody. Do something.

Norman Vincent Peale

You will always have joy in the evening if you spend the day fruitfully.

Thomas à Kempis

*Be strong and brave, and do the work.
Don't be afraid or discouraged, because the Lord God, my God, is with you. He will not fail you or leave you.*

1 Chronicles 28:20 NCV

An idle life and a holy heart are a contradiction.

Thomas Brooks

The higher the ideal, the more work is required to accomplish it.
Do not expect to become a great success in life
if you are not willing to work for it.

Father Flanagan

More Words from God's Word

Each of us will be rewarded for his own hard work.

1 Corinthians 3:8 TLB

Do all you can to live a peaceful life. Take care of your own business, and do your own work as we have already told you. If you do, then people who are not believers will respect you, and you will not have to depend on others for what you need.

1 Thessalonians 4:11-12 NCV

He did it with all his heart, and prospered.

2 Chronicles 31:21 KJV

Now this I say, he who sows sparingly will also reap sparingly, and he who sows bountifully will also reap bountifully.

2 Corinthians 9:6 NASB

My Values for Life

	Check Your Value		
	High	Med.	Low
The importance that I place on the need to work diligently, consistently, and enthusiastically . . .	___	___	___
The value of associating with hardworking, enthusiastic people . . .	___	___	___
The value that I place on knowing that I'm personally responsible for the quality of my work . . .	___	___	___

Accepting the Gift of Grace

For by grace you have been saved through faith,
and that not of yourselves; it is the gift of God,
not of works, lest anyone should boast.

Ephesians 2:8-9 NKJV

God's grace is not earned . . . thank goodness! To earn God's love and His gift of eternal life would be far beyond the abilities of even the most righteous man or woman. Thankfully, grace is not an earthly reward for righteous behavior; it is a blessed spiritual gift which can be accepted by believers who dedicate themselves to God through Christ. When we accept Christ into our hearts, we are saved by His grace.

The familiar words of Ephesians 2:8 make God's promise perfectly clear: It is by grace we have been saved, through faith. We are saved not because of our good deeds but because of our faith in Christ.

God's grace is the ultimate gift, and we owe to Him the ultimate in thanksgiving. Let us praise the Creator for His priceless gift, and let us share the Good News with all who cross our paths. We return our Father's love by accepting His grace and by sharing His message and His love.

Have you thanked God today for blessings that are too numerous to count? Have you offered Him your heartfelt prayers and your wholehearted praise? If not, it's time to slow down and offer a prayer of thanksgiving to the One who has given you life on earth and life eternal.

If you are a thoughtful Christian, you will be a thankful Christian. No matter your circumstances, you owe God so much more than you can ever repay, and you owe Him your heartfelt thanks. So thank Him . . . and keep thanking Him, today, tomorrow, and forever.

Jesus has affected human society like no other.
The incomparable Christ is the good news.
And what makes it such good news is that man is so undeserving
but that God is so gracious.

John MacArthur

Values for Life

God's grace is always available: Jim Cymbala writes, "No one is beyond his grace. No situation, anywhere on earth, is too hard for God." If you sincerely seek God's grace, He will give it freely. So ask, and you will receive.

Timeless Wisdom for Godly Living

The grace of God is sufficient for all our needs,
for every problem, and for every difficulty, for every broken heart,
and for every human sorrow.

Peter Marshall

Let us, then, feel very sure that we can come before God's throne where there is grace. There we can receive mercy and grace to help us when we need it.

Hebrews 4:16 NCV

To believe is to take freely what God gives freely.

C. H. Spurgeon

The grace of God is infinite and eternal. As it had no beginning,
so it can have no end, and being an attribute of God,
it is as boundless as infinitude.

A. W. Tozer

The grace of God transcends all our feeble efforts to describe it.
It cannot be poured into any mental receptacle without running over.

Vance Havner

Grace: a gift that costs everything for the giver and
nothing for the recipient.

Philip Yancey

More Words from God's Word

Grace to you and peace from God our Father and the Lord Jesus Christ.

Philippians 1:2 NASB

My grace is sufficient for you, for my power is made perfect in weakness.

2 Corinthians 12:9 NIV

You therefore, my son, be strong in the grace that is in Christ Jesus.

2 Timothy 2:1 NKJV

Therefore let us approach the throne of grace with boldness, so that we may receive mercy and find grace to help us at the proper time.

Hebrews 4:16 HCSB

But God gives us even more grace, as the Scripture says, "God is against the proud, but he gives grace to the humble."

James 4:6 NCV

My Values for Life

	Check Your Value		
	High	Med.	Low
God's gifts to me are treasures upon which I place . . .	___	___	___
The importance of sharing the transforming message of God's gift of grace . . .	___	___	___
The value that I place upon God's promise that His grace is sufficient for my needs . . .	___	___	___

Value-based Decisions

Depend on the Lord in whatever you do, and your plans will succeed.

Proverbs 16:3 NCV

Life is a series of choices. From the instant we wake in the morning until the moment we nod off to sleep at night, we make countless decisions: decisions about the things we do, decisions about the words we speak, and decisions about the thoughts we choose to think. Simply put, the quality of those decisions determines the quality of our lives.

Some decisions are easy to make because the consequences of those decisions are small. When the person behind the counter asks, "Want fries with that?" the necessary response requires little thought because the consequences of that decision are minor.

Some decisions, on the other hand, are big . . . *very* big. The biggest decision, of course, is one that far too many people ignore: the decision concerning God's only begotten Son. But if you're a believer in Christ, you've already made that choice, and you have received God's gift of grace. Perhaps now you're asking yourself, "What's next, Lord?" If so, you may be facing a series of big decisions concerning your life and your future. Here are some things you can do:

1. Gather as much information as you can: don't expect to get all the facts—that's impossible—but get as many facts as you can in a reasonable amount of time. (Proverbs 24:3-4)
2. Don't be too impulsive: If you have time to make a decision, use that time to make a good decision. (Proverbs 19:2)

3. Rely on the advice of trusted friends and mentors. Proverbs 1:5 makes it clear: "A wise man will hear and increase learning, and a man of understanding will attain wise counsel" (NKJV).
4. Pray for guidance. When you seek it, He will give it. (Luke 11:9)
5. Make choices based upon values not convenience: Trust the quiet inner voice of your conscience: Treat your conscience as you would a trusted advisor. (Luke 17:21)
6. When the time for action arrives, act. Procrastination is the enemy of progress; don't let it defeat you. (James 1:22)

As we trust God to give us wisdom for today's decisions,
He will lead us a step at a time into
what He wants us to be doing in the future.

Theodore Epp

Values for Life

Slow Down! If you're about to make an important decision, don't be impulsive. Remember: big decisions have big consequences, and if you don't think about those consequences now, you may pay a big price later.

Timeless Wisdom for Godly Living

Never make a decision without stopping to consider the matter in the presence of God.

Josemaria Escriva

When we learn to listen to Christ's voice for the details of our daily decisions, we begin to know Him personally.

Catherine Marshall

I am offering you life or death, blessings or curses. Now, choose life! . . . To choose life is to love the Lord your God, obey him, and stay close to him.

Deuteronomy 30:19-20 NCV

Good and evil both increase at compound interest. That is why the little decisions you and I make every day are of such infinite importance.

C. S. *Lewis*

If you are struggling to make some difficult decisions right now that aren't specifically addressed in the Bible, don't make a choice based on what's right for someone else. You are the LORD's and He will make sure you do what's right.

Lisa Whelchel

More Words from God's Word

Now it happened as they went that He entered a certain village; and a certain woman named Martha welcomed Him into her house. And she had a sister called Mary, who also sat at Jesus' feet and heard His word. But Martha was distracted with much serving, and she approached Him and said, "Lord, do You not care that my sister has left me to serve alone? Therefore tell her to help me." And Jesus answered and said to her, "Martha, Martha, you are worried and troubled about many things. But one thing is needed, and Mary has chosen that good part, which will not be taken away from her."

Luke 10:38-42 NKJV

The thing you should want most is God's kingdom and doing what God wants. Then all these other things you need will be given to you.

Matthew 6:33 NCV

But Daniel purposed in his heart that he would not defile himself . . . .

Daniel 1:8 KJV

My Values for Life

	Check Your Value		
	High	Med.	Low
In making important decisions, the value that I place upon God's guidance is . . .	___	___	___
The importance of making decisions based upon the teachings of God's Word . . .	___	___	___
The need that I feel to be accountable for the decisions I make . . .	___	___	___

Trusting His Timetable

I trust in You, O Lord, I say, "You are my God."
My times are in Your hand.

Psalm 31:14-15 NASB

We human beings are, by our very nature, impatient. We are impatient with others, impatient with ourselves, and impatient with our Creator. We want things to happen according to our own timetables, but our Heavenly Father may have other plans. That's why we must learn the art of patience.

All too often, we are unwilling to trust God's perfect timing. We allow ourselves to become apprehensive and anxious as we wait nervously for God to act. Usually, we know what we want, and we know precisely when we want it: right now, if not sooner. But, when God's plans differ from our own, we must train ourselves to trust in His infinite wisdom and in His infinite love.

As busy men and women living in a fast-paced world, many of us find that waiting quietly for God is quite troubling. But in our better moments, we realize that patience is not only a virtue; it is also a commandment from the Creator.

Psalm 37:7 makes it clear that we should "Be still before the Lord and wait patiently for Him" (NIV). But ours is a generation that usually places little value on stillness and patience. No matter. God instructs us to be patient in all things, and we must obey Him or suffer the consequences of His displeasure.

We must be patient with our families, with our friends, with our associates, and with ourselves. We must also be patient with our Heavenly Father as He shapes our world (and our lives) in accordance with His timetable, not our own. And that's as it should be. After all, think how patient God has been with us.

Grass that is here today and gone tomorrow does not require much time to mature. A big oak tree that lasts for generations requires much more time to grow and mature. God is concerned about your life through eternity. Allow Him to take all the time He needs to shape you for His purposes. Larger assignments will require longer periods of preparation.

Henry Blackaby

Values for Life

Trust God's Timing. God has very big plans in store for you, so trust Him and wait patiently for those plans to unfold. And remember: God's timing is best, so don't allow yourself to become discouraged if things don't work out exactly as you wish. Instead of worrying about your future, entrust it to God. He knows exactly what you need and exactly when you need it.

Timeless Wisdom for Godly Living

When there is perplexity there is always guidance—not always at the moment we ask, but in good time, which is God's time. There is no need to fret and stew.

Elisabeth Elliot

Humble yourselves, therefore, under God's mighty hand, that he may lift you up in due time.

1 Peter 5:6 NIV

That time spent in waiting for a promise to be fulfilled is when faith envisions the outcome. It's in that gap that we can delight God. Without this kind of faith, it's impossible to please God (Hebrews 11:6).

Franklin Graham

Even Jesus, clear as he was about his calling,
had to get his instructions one day at a time.
One time he was told to wait, another time to go.

Laurie Beth Jones

The stops of a good man are ordered by the Lord as well as his steps.

George Mueller

Waiting is an essential part of spiritual discipline.
It can be the ultimate test of faith.

Anne Graham Lotz

More Words from God's Word

From one man he made every nation of men, that they should inhabit the whole earth; and he determined the times set for them and the exact places where they should live.

Acts 17:26 NIV

He has made everything beautiful in its time. He has also set eternity in the hearts of men; yet they cannot fathom what God has done from beginning to end.

Ecclesiastes 3:11 NIV

So teach us to number our days, that we may gain a heart of wisdom.

Psalm 90:12 NKJV

He [Jesus] said to them: "It is not for you to know the times or dates the Father has set by his own authority."

Acts 1:7 NIV

My Values for Life

	Check Your Value		
	High	Med.	Low
Accepting God's will (even when I don't understand it) has a value that is . . .	___	___	___
I am willing to wait patiently for God to respond to my prayers . . .	___	___	___
My trust in God has a value to me that is . . .	___	___	___

And the Greatest of These . . .

Now these three remain: faith, hope, and love.
But the greatest of these is love.

1 Corinthians 13:13 HCSB

Love is a choice. Either you choose to behave lovingly toward others . . . or not; either you behave yourself in ways that enhance your relationships . . . or not. But make no mistake: genuine love requires effort. Simply put, if you wish to build lasting relationships, you must be willing to do your part.

Since the days of Adam and Eve, God has allowed His children to make choices for themselves, and so it is with you. As you interact with family and friends, you have choices to make . . . lots of them. If you choose wisely, you'll be rewarded; if you choose unwisely, you'll bear the consequences.

Christ's words are clear: we are to love God first, and secondly, we are to love others as we love ourselves (Matthew 22:37-40). These two commands are seldom easy, and because we are imperfect beings, we often fall short. But God's Holy Word commands us to try.

The Christian path is an exercise in love and forgiveness. If we are to walk in Christ's footsteps, we must forgive those who have done us harm, and we must accept Christ's love by sharing it freely with family, friends, neighbors, and even strangers.

God does not intend for you to experience mediocre

relationships; He created you for far greater things. Building lasting relationships requires compassion, wisdom, empathy, kindness, courtesy, and forgiveness. If that sounds like work, it is—which is perfectly fine with God. Why? Because He knows that you are capable of doing that work, and because He knows that the fruits of your labors will enrich the lives of your loved ones and the lives of generations yet unborn.

So Jesus came, stripping himself of everything as he came—omnipotence, omniscience, omnipresence—everything except love. "He emptied himself" (Philippians 2:7), emptied himself of everything except love. Love—his only protection, his only weapon, his only method.

E. Stanley Jones

Values for Life

Do you want love to last? Then you must understand this: Genuine love requires effort. That's why those who are lazy in love are often losers in love, too!

Timeless Wisdom for Godly Living

You will find, as you look back upon your life,
that the moments when you have really lived are the moments
when you have done things in the spirit of love.

Henry Drummond

It is important to know that you have to work to keep love alive;
you have to protect it and maintain it,
just like you would a delicate flower.

James Dobson

The truth of the Gospel is intended to free us to love God
and others with our whole heart.

John Eldredge

*Dear friends, since God loved us that much,
we surely ought to love each other.*

1 John 4:11 NLT

He who loves brings God and the world together.

Martin Buber

Be faithful in the little practices of love which will build in you
the life of holiness and will make you Christlike.

Mother Teresa

More Words from God's Word

Love one another earnestly from a pure heart.

1 Peter 1:22 HCSB

May the Lord cause you to increase and abound in love for one another, and for all people.

1 Thessalonians 3:12 NASB

And the most important piece of clothing you must wear is love. Love is what binds us all together in perfect harmony.

Colossians 3:14 NLT

A new commandment I give to you, that you love one another; as I have loved you, that you also love one another.

John 13:34 NKJV

My Values for Life

	Check Your Value		
	High	Med.	Low
As a follower of Christ, I understand that I am commanded to love other people, and I take that commandment seriously . . .	___	___	___
Because I place a high priority on my relationships, I am willing to invest the time and energy that are required to make those relationships work . . .	___	___	___
When I have been hurt by someone, I understand the importance of forgiving that person as quickly as possible *and* as completely as possible . . .	___	___	___

Behaviors That Are Pleasing to Whom?

Do you think I am trying to make people accept me? No, God is the One I am trying to please. Am I trying to please people? If I still wanted to please people, I would not be a servant of Christ.

Galatians 1:10 NCV

Whom will you try to please today: God or man? Your primary obligation, of course, is to please your Father in heaven not your friends in the neighborhood. But even if you're a devoted Christian, you may, from time to time, feel the urge to impress your peers—and sometimes that urge can be strong.

Peer pressure can be a good thing or a bad thing, depending upon your peers. If your peers encourage you to follow God's will and to obey His commandments, then you'll experience positive peer pressure, and that's good. But, if you are involved with friends who encourage you to do foolish things, you're facing a different kind of peer pressure . . . and you'd better beware. When you feel pressured to do things—or to say things—that lead you away from God, you're aiming straight for trouble. So don't do the "easy" thing or the "popular" thing. Do the right thing, and don't worry about winning popularity contests.

Here are a few things to remember about peer pressure:

1. Peer pressure exists, and you will experience it.
2. If your peers encourage you to behave yourself, to honor God, and to become a better person, peer pressure can

actually be a good thing . . . up to a point. But remember: you don't have to be perfect to be wonderful. So if you're trying to be perfect, lighten up on yourself, and while you're at it, lighten up on others, too.

3. If your friends are encouraging you to misbehave or underachieve, find new friends. Today.

Rick Warren correctly observed, "Those who follow the crowd usually get lost in it." Are you satisfied to follow that crowd? If so, you will probably pay a heavy price for your shortsightedness. But if you're determined to follow the One from Galilee, He will guide your steps and bless your undertakings. To sum it up, here's your choice: you can choose to please God first, or you can fall prey to peer pressure. The choice is yours—and so are the consequences.

You will get untold flak for prioritizing God's revealed and present will for your life over man's . . . but, boy, is it worth it.

Beth Moore

Values for Life

Put peer pressure to work for you: How? By associating with people who, by their actions and their words, will encourage you to become a better person.

Timeless Wisdom for Godly Living

There is nothing that makes more cowards and feeble men than public opinion.

Henry Ward Beecher

When we are set free from the bondage of pleasing others, when we are free from currying others' favor and others' approval—then no one will be able to make us miserable or dissatisfied. And then, if we know we have pleased God, contentment will be our consolation.

Kay Arthur

Blessed is the man who does not walk in the counsel of the wicked or stand in the way of sinners or sit in the seat of mockers. But his delight is in the law of the LORD, and on his law he meditates day and night. He is like a tree planted by streams of water, which yields its fruit in season and whose leaf does not wither. Whatever he does prospers.

Psalm 1:1-3 NIV

It is comfortable to know that we are responsible to God and not to man. It is a small matter to be judged of man's judgement.

Lottie Moon

If you try to be everything to everybody, you will end up being nothing to anybody.

Vance Havner

More Words from God's Word

He who walks with the wise grows wise,
but a companion of fools suffers harm.

Proverbs 13:20 NIV

Therefore, whether we are at home or away, we make it our aim to be pleasing to Him. For we must all appear before the judgment seat of Christ, so that each may be repaid for what he has done in the body, whether good or bad.

2 Corinthians 5:9-10 HCSB

May the words of my mouth and the thoughts of my heart be pleasing to you, O Lord, my rock and my redeemer.

Psalm 19:14 NLT

Do not conform any longer to the pattern of this world, but be transformed by the renewing of your mind. Then you will be able to test and approve what God's will is—his good, pleasing and perfect will.

Romans 12:2 NIV

My Values for Life

Statement	Check Your Value: High	Med.	Low
The value that I place upon pleasing God is . . .	___	___	___
I actively seek out wise friends who help me make right choices . . .	___	___	___
Being obedient to God means that I cannot always please other people . . .	___	___	___

The Right Kind of Fear

The fear of the Lord *is a fountain of life . . . .*

Proverbs 14:27 NIV

Are you a Christian who possesses a healthy, fearful respect for God's power? Hopefully so. After all, God's Word teaches that the fear of the Lord is the beginning of knowledge (Proverbs 1:7).

When you fear the Creator—and when you honor Him by obeying His commandments—you will receive God's approval and His blessings. But, if you ignore Him or disobey His commandments, you invite disastrous consequences.

God's hand shapes the universe, and it shapes our lives. God maintains absolute sovereignty over His creation, and His power is beyond comprehension. As believers, we must cultivate a sincere respect for God's awesome power. The fear of the Lord is, indeed, the surest form of wisdom.

In the book of Exodus, God warns that we should place no gods before Him. Yet all too often, we place our Lord in second, third, or fourth place as we worship the gods of pride, greed, power, or lust.

When we place our desires for material possessions above our love for God—or when we yield to temptations of the flesh—we find ourselves engaged in a struggle that is similar to the one Jesus faced when He was tempted by Satan. In the wilderness, Satan offered Jesus earthly power and unimaginable riches, but Jesus turned Satan away and chose instead to worship God. We must seek to imitate Christ by putting God first and worshipping only Him.

Is God your top priority? Have you given His Son your heart, your soul, your talents, and your time? Or are you in the habit of giving God little more than a few hours on Sunday morning? The answer to these questions will determine how you prioritize your days and your life.

So today, as you face the realities of everyday life, remember this: until you acquire a healthy fear of God's power, your education is incomplete, and so is your faith.

The fear of God is the death of every other fear.

C. H. *Spurgeon*

Values for Life

It's the right kind of fear . . . Your respect for God should make you fearful of disobeying Him . . . *very* fearful.

Timeless Wisdom for Godly Living

A healthy fear of God will do much to deter us from sin.

Charles Swindoll

The fear of the LORD is the beginning of knowledge,
but fools despise wisdom and discipline.

Proverbs 1:7 NIV

Remember that this fear of the Lord is His treasure, a choice jewel,
given only to favorites, and to those who are greatly beloved.

John Bunyan

The remarkable thing about fearing God is that when you fear God,
you fear nothing else, whereas if you do not fear God,
you fear everything else.

Oswald Chambers

If we do not tremble before God,
the world's system seems wonderful to us and pleasantly consumes us.

James Montgomery Boice

There will be no true freedom without virtue,
no true science without religion, no true industry
without the fear of God and love to your fellow citizens.

Charles Kingsley

More Words from God's Word

Fear the LORD your God, serve him only and take your oaths in his name.

Deuteronomy 6:13 NIV

The reward of humility and the fear of the LORD are riches, honor and life.

Proverbs 22:4 NASB

How blessed is everyone who fears the LORD, who walks in His ways.

Psalm 128:1 NASB

"Fear God and give Him glory, because the hour of His judgment has come. Worship the Maker of heaven and earth, the sea and springs of water."

Revelation 14:7 HCSB

For the LORD your God is God of gods and Lord of lords, the great God, mighty and awesome.

Deuteronomy 10:17 NIV

My Values for Life

Statement	Check Your Value: High	Med.	Low
I believe that it is important to have a healthy respect for God's power.	___	___	___
I have a healthy fear of disobeying God.	___	___	___
I think that it is important to find ways to worship God throughout the day.	___	___	___

The Cheerful Giver

So let each one give as he purposes in his heart,
not grudgingly or of necessity; for God loves a cheerful giver.
2 Corinthians 9:7 NKJV

The thread of generosity is woven—completely and inextricably—into the very fabric of Christ's teachings. As He sent His disciples out to heal the sick and spread God's message of salvation, Jesus offered this guiding principle: "Freely you have received, freely give" (Matthew 10:8 NIV). The principle still applies. If we are to be disciples of Christ, we must give freely of our time, our possessions, and our love.

In 2 Corinthians 9, Paul reminds us that when we sow the seeds of generosity, we reap bountiful rewards in accordance with God's plan for our lives. Thus, we are instructed to give cheerfully and without reservation: "But this I say, He which soweth sparingly shall reap also sparingly; and he which soweth bountifully shall reap also bountifully. Every man according as he purposeth in his heart, so let him give; not grudgingly, or of necessity: for God loveth a cheerful giver" (vv. 6, 7 KJV).

Are you a cheerful giver? If you intend to obey God's commandments, you must be. When you give, God looks not only at the quality of your gift but also at the condition of your heart. If you give generously, joyfully, and without complaint, you obey God's Word. But, if you make your gifts grudgingly, or if the motivation for your gift is selfish, you invite God's displeasure.

One of life's greatest joys is the ability to share your gifts with others. The more you earn and save, the more you'll have to share. So today, make this pledge and keep it: Be a cheerful, generous, courageous giver. The world needs your help, and you need the spiritual rewards that will be yours when you do.

Nothing is really ours until we share it.

C. S. Lewis

Values for Life

Would you like to be a little happier? Try sharing a few more of the blessings that God has bestowed upon you. In other words, if you want to be happy, be generous. And if you want to be unhappy, be greedy.

Timeless Wisdom for Godly Living

We are never more like God than when we give.

Charles Swindoll

The happiest and most joyful people are those
who give money and serve.

Dave Ramsey

The world says, the more you take, the more you have.
Christ says, the more you give, the more you are.

Frederick Buechner

A cheerful giver does not count the cost of what he gives.
His heart is set on pleasing and cheering him
to whom the gift is given.

Juliana of Norwich

A cup that is already full cannot have more added to it.
In order to receive the further good to which we are entitled,
we must give of that which we have.

Margaret Becker

I have shown you in every way, by laboring like this,
that you must support the weak.
And remember the words of the Lord Jesus, that He said,
"It is more blessed to give than to receive."

Acts 20:35 NKJV

More Words from God's Word

Whenever we have the opportunity, we should do good to everyone, especially to our Christian brothers and sisters.

Galatians 6:10 NLT

Let us not lose heart in doing good, for in due time we shall reap if we do not grow weary. So then, while we have opportunity, let us do good to all men, and especially to those who are of the household of the faith.

Galatians 6:9-10 NASB

The man with two tunics should share with him who has none, and the one who has food should do the same.

Luke 3:11 NIV

My Values for Life

	Check Your Value		
	High	Med.	Low
Because I have been blessed by God, it is important for me to share my blessings with others . . .	___	___	___
I believe that a direct relationship exists between generosity and joy—the more I give the more joy I experience . . .	___	___	___
Jesus Christ gave His life for me; His selfless act motivates me to be a selfless giver . . .	___	___	___

The Courage to Dream

But as for me, I will always have hope; I will praise you more and more.
Psalm 71:14 NIV

Are you willing to entertain the possibility that God has big plans in store for you? Hopefully so. Yet sometimes, especially if you've recently experienced a life-altering disappointment, you may find it difficult to envision a brighter future for yourself and your family. If so, it's time to reconsider your own capabilities . . . and God's.

Your Heavenly Father created you with unique gifts and untapped talents; your job is to tap them. When you do, you'll begin to feel an increasing sense of confidence in yourself and in your future. As the old saying goes, if you feed your faith, your doubts will starve to death.

On occasion, you will face the inevitable disappointments of life. And sometimes, you must endure life-altering personal losses that leave you breathless. On such occasions, you may be tempted to abandon your dreams. Don't do it! Instead, trust that God is preparing you for greater things.

Concentration camp survivor Corrie ten Boom observed, "Every experience God gives us, every person he brings into our lives, is the perfect preparation for the future that only he can see." These words apply to you.

Are you excited about the opportunities of today and thrilled by the possibilities of tomorrow? Do you confidently expect God to lead you to a place of abundance, peace, and joy? And, when your days on earth are over, do you expect to receive the priceless gift of eternal life? If you trust God's promises, and if you have welcomed God's Son into your heart, then you believe that your future is intensely and eternally bright.

It takes courage to dream big dreams. You will discover that courage when you do three things: accept the past, trust God to handle the future, and make the most of the time He has given you today.

Nothing is too difficult for God, and no dreams are too big for Him—not even yours. So start living—and dreaming—accordingly.

The future lies all before us. Shall it only be a slight advance upon what we usually do? Ought it not to be a bound, a leap forward to altitudes of endeavor and success undreamed of before?

Annie Armstrong

Values for Life

Making your dreams come true requires work. John Maxwell writes, "The gap between your vision and your present reality can only be filled through a commitment to maximize your potential." Enough said.

Timeless Wisdom for Godly Living

Always stay connected to people and seek out things that bring you joy. Dream with abandon. Pray confidently.

Barbara Johnson

Sometimes our dreams were so big that it took two people to dream them.

Marie T. Freeman

We must be willing to give up every dream but God's dream.

Larry Crabb

May he grant your heart's desire and fulfill all your plans.

Psalm 20:4 NLT

Dreaming the dream of God is not for cowards.

Joey Johnson

To make your dream come true, you have to stay awake.

Dennis Swanberg

More Words from God's Word

Where there is no vision, the people perish . . . .

Proverbs 29:18 KJV

I came so they can have real and eternal life,
more and better life than they ever dreamed of.

John 10:10 MSG

May He grant you according to your heart's desire,
and fulfill all your purpose.

Psalm 20:4 NKJV

Trust in the LORD with all your heart;
do not depend on your own understanding.

Proverbs 3:5 NLT

For with God nothing will be impossible.

Luke 1:37 NKJV

My Values for Life

	Check Your Value		
	High	Med.	Low
For me, having big dreams and lofty goals is	___	___	___
I trust that God's dream for my life is better than anything I could possibly dream up on my own . . .	___	___	___
For me, the quest to fulfill my dreams is a continuing journey, not a final destination . . .	___	___	___

Valuing God's Guidance

In all your ways acknowledge Him, and He shall direct your paths.

Proverbs 3:6 NKJV

When we genuinely seek to know the heart of God—when we prayerfully seek His wisdom and His will—our Heavenly Father carefully guides us over the peaks and valleys of life. And as Christians, we can be comforted: Whether we find ourselves at the pinnacle of the mountain or the darkest depths of the valley, the loving heart of God is always there with us.

As Christians whose salvation has been purchased by the blood of Christ, we have every reason to live joyously and courageously. After all, Christ has already fought and won our battle for us—He did so on the cross at Calvary. But despite Christ's sacrifice, and despite God's promises, we may become confused or disoriented by the endless complications and countless distractions of life here in the 21st century.

C. S. Lewis observed, "I don't doubt that the Holy Spirit guides your decisions from within when you make them with the intention of pleasing God. The error would be to think that He speaks only within, whereas in reality He speaks also through Scripture, the Church, Christian friends, and books." These words remind us that God has many ways to make Himself known. Our challenge is to make *ourselves* open to His instruction.

Do you place a high value on God's guidance, and do you talk to Him regularly about matters great and small? Or do you talk with God on a haphazard basis? If you're wise, you'll form the habit of speaking to God early and often. But you won't stop there—you'll also study God's Word, you'll obey God's commandments, and you'll associate with people who do likewise.

So, if you're unsure of your next step, lean upon God's promises and lift your prayers to Him. Remember that God is always near—always trying to get His message through. Open yourself to Him every day, and trust Him to guide your path. When you do, you'll be protected today, tomorrow, and forever.

A spiritual discipline is necessary in order to move slowly from an absurd to an obedient life, from a life filled with noisy worries to a life in which there is some free inner space where we can listen to our God and follow his guidance.

Henri Nouwen

Values for Life

Pray for guidance. When you seek it, He will give it. (Luke 11:9)

Timeless Wisdom for Godly Living

God will prove to you how good and acceptable and perfect His will is when He's got His hands on the steering wheel of your life.

Stuart & Jill Briscoe

The Bible is not a guidebook to a theological museum. It is a road map showing us the way into neglected or even forgotten glories of the living God.

Raymond Ortlund

Men give advice; God gives guidance.

Leonard Ravenhill

It's a bit like river rafting with an experienced guide. You may begin to panic when the guide steers you straight into a steep waterfall, especially if another course appears much safer. Yet, after you've emerged from the swirling depths and wiped the spray from your eyes, you see that just beyond the seemingly "safe" route was a series of jagged rocks. Your guide knew what he was doing after all.

Shirley Dobson

I will instruct you and teach you in the way you should go; I will guide you with My eye.

Psalm 32:8 NKJV

More Words from God's Word

The true children of God are those who let God's Spirit lead them.

Romans 8:14 NCV

In thee, O LORD, do I put my trust; let me never be put into confusion.

Psalm 71:1 KJV

Our God forever and ever . . . will guide us until death.

Psalm 48:14 NASB

Every morning he wakes me. He teaches me to listen like a student. The Lord God helps me learn . . . .

Isaiah 50:4-5 NCV

Teach me Your way, O LORD, and lead me in a level path.

Psalm 27:11 NASB

My Values for Life

	Check Your Value		
	High	Med.	Low
In making decisions, the value that I place upon God's wisdom is . . .	___	___	___
I allow God to guide me by His Word and by His Spirit . . .	___	___	___
When I genuinely trust God to guide my path, I am comforted . . .	___	___	___

Accepting God's Abundance

I have come that they may have life,
and that they may have it more abundantly.

John 10:10 NKJV

God's gifts are available to all, but they are not guaranteed; those gifts must be claimed by those who choose to follow Christ. As believers, we are free to accept God's gifts, or not; that choice, and the consequences that result from it, are ours and ours alone.

The 10th chapter of John tells us that Christ came to earth so that our lives might be filled with abundance. But what, exactly, did Jesus mean when He promised "life . . . more abundantly"? Was Jesus referring to material possessions or financial wealth? Hardly. When Jesus declared Himself the shepherd of mankind (John 10:7-9), He offered a different kind of abundance: a spiritual richness that extends beyond the temporal boundaries of this world.

If you are a thoughtful believer, you will open yourself to Christ's spiritual abundance by following Him completely and without reservation. When you do, you will receive the love, the peace, and the joy that He has promised.

The fullness of life in Christ is available to all who seek it and claim it. Count yourself among that number. Seek first the salvation that is available through a personal relationship with Jesus, and then claim the abundance that can—and should—be yours.

Do you sincerely seek the riches that our Savior offers to those who give themselves to Him? Then follow Him—and receive the blessings that He has promised. When you establish an intimate, passionate relationship with Christ, you are then free to claim the love, the protection, and the spiritual abundance that the Shepherd offers His sheep.

> The gift of God is eternal life, spiritual life,
> abundant life through faith in Jesus Christ,
> the Living Word of God.
>
> *Anne Graham Lotz*

Values for Life

Don't miss out on God's abundance: Every day is a beautifully wrapped gift from God. Unwrap it; use it; and give thanks to the Giver.

Timeless Wisdom for Godly Living

The man who lives without Jesus is the poorest of the poor, whereas no one is so rich as the man who lives in His grace.

Thomas à Kempis

God has promised us abundance, peace, and eternal life. These treasures are ours for the asking; all we must do is claim them. One of the great mysteries of life is why on earth do so many of us wait so very long to lay claim to God's gifts?

Marie T. Freeman

My cup runs over. Surely goodness and mercy shall follow me all the days of my life; and I will dwell in the house of the LORD Forever.

Psalm 23:5-6 NKJV

People, places, and things were never meant to give us life. God alone is the author of a fulfilling life.

Gary Smalley & John Trent

Instead of living a black-and-white existence, we'll be released into a technicolor world of vibrancy and emotion when we more accurately reflect His nature to the world around us.

Bill Hybels

More Words from God's Word

Now this I say, he who sows sparingly will also reap sparingly,
and he who sows bountifully will also reap bountifully.

2 Corinthians 9:6 NASB

If you give, you will receive. Your gift will return to you in full measure,
pressed down, shaken together to make room for more,
and running over. Whatever measure you use in giving—large or small—
it will be used to measure what is given back to you.

Luke 6:38 NLT

And God is able to make all grace abound to you,
so that always having all sufficiency in everything,
you may have an abundance for every good deed . . . .

2 Corinthians 9:8 NASB

My Values for Life

Statement	Check Your Value: High	Med.	Low
Abundant living may or may not include material wealth, but abundant living always includes the spiritual riches that I receive when I obey God's Word . . .	___	___	___
I understand the importance of thanking God for gifts that are simply too numerous to count . . .	___	___	___
For me, to follow Christ is to live abundantly . . .	___	___	___

The Value of Doing What Needs to Be Done

Are there those among you who are truly wise and understanding? Then they should show it by living right and doing good things with a gentleness that comes from wisdom.

James 3:13 NCV

The old saying is both familiar and true: actions speak louder than words. And as believers, we must beware: our actions should always give credence to the changes that Christ can make in the lives of those who walk with Him.

God calls upon each of us to act in accordance with His will and with respect for His commandments. If we are to be responsible believers, we must realize that it is never enough to hear the instructions of God; we must also live by them. And it is never enough to wait idly by while others do God's work here on earth; we, too, must act. Doing God's work is a responsibility that each of us must bear, and when we do, our loving Heavenly Father rewards our efforts with a bountiful harvest.

Are you in the habit of doing what needs to be done when it needs to be done, or are you a dues-paying member of the Procrastinator's Club? If you've acquired the habit of doing things sooner rather than later, congratulations! But, if you find yourself putting off all those unpleasant tasks until later (or never), it's time to think about the consequences of your behavior.

One way that you can learn to defeat procrastination is by paying less attention to your fears and more attention to your responsibilities. So, when you're faced with a difficult choice or an unpleasant responsibility, don't spend endless hours fretting over your fate. Simply seek God's counsel and get busy. When you do, you will be richly rewarded because of your willingness to act.

Do noble things; do not dream them all day long.

Charles Kingsley

Values for Life

If unpleasant work needs to be done, do it sooner rather than later . . . It's easy to put off unpleasant tasks until "later." A far better strategy is this: Do the unpleasant work first so you can enjoy the rest of the day.

Timeless Wisdom for Godly Living

If doing a good act in public will excite others to do more good, then "Let your Light shine to all." Miss no opportunity to do good.

John Wesley

Let us not be content to wait and see what will happen, but give us the determination to make the right things happen.

Peter Marshall

The church needs people who are doers of the Word and not just hearers.

Warren Wiersbe

Logic will not change an emotion, but action will.

Zig Ziglar

Therefore, get your minds ready for action, being self-disciplined, and set your hope completely on the grace to be brought to you at the revelation of Jesus Christ. As obedient children, do not be conformed to the desires of your former ignorance but, as the One who called you is holy, you also are to be holy in all your conduct.

1 Peter 1:13-15 HCSB

Action

More Words from God's Word

Are there those among you who are truly wise and understanding? Then they should show it by living right and doing good things with a gentleness that comes from wisdom.

James 3:13 NCV

For God is working in you, giving you the desire to obey him and the power to do what pleases him.

Philippians 2:13 NLT

Blessed are they who maintain justice, who constantly do what is right.

Psalm 106:3 NIV

For it is not merely knowing the law that brings God's approval. Those who obey the law will be declared right in God's sight.

Romans 2:13 NLT

My Values for Life

	Check Your Value		
	High	Med.	Low
When God speaks to me, I listen, and I go to work . . .	___	___	___
I believe that my testimony is more powerful when actions accompany my words . . .	___	___	___
I see the hypocrisy in saying one thing and doing another, so I do my best to act in accordance with my beliefs . . .	___	___	___

The High Value of High Praise

I will praise the LORD at all times, I will constantly speak his praises.

Psalm 34:1 NLT

When is the best time to praise God? In church? Before dinner is served? When we tuck little children into bed? None of the above. The best time to praise God is all day, every day, to the greatest extent we can, with thanksgiving in our hearts and with a song on our lips.

Too many of us, even well-intentioned believers, tend to "compartmentalize" our waking hours into a few familiar categories: work, rest, play, family time, and worship. To do so is a mistake. Worship and praise should be woven into the fabric of everything we do; it should never be relegated to a weekly three-hour visit to church on Sunday morning.

The words by Fanny Crosby are familiar: "This is my story, this is my song, praising my Savior, all the day long." As believers who have been saved by the sacrifice of a risen Christ, we must do exactly as the song instructs: We must praise our Savior time and time again throughout the day. Worship and praise should be a part of everything we do. Otherwise, we quickly lose perspective as we fall prey to the demands of everyday life.

Theologian Wayne Oates once admitted, "Many of my prayers are made with my eyes open. You see, it seems I'm always praying about something, and it's not always convenient—or safe—to close my eyes." Dr. Oates understood that God always hears our prayers and that the relative position of our eyelids is of no concern to Him.

Do you sincerely desire to be a worthy servant of the One who has given you eternal love and eternal life? Then praise Him for who He is and for what He has done for you. And don't just praise Him on Sunday morning. Praise Him all day long, every day, for as long as you live . . . and then for all eternity.

Praising God is one of the highest and purest acts of religion.
In prayer we act like men; in praise we act like angels.

Thomas Watson

Values for Life

Praise Him! One of the main reasons you go to church is to praise God. But, you need not wait until Sunday rolls around to thank your Heavenly Father. Instead, you can praise Him many times each day by saying silent prayers that only He can hear.

Timeless Wisdom for Godly Living

Praising God reduces your cares, levels your anxieties, and multiplies your blessings.

Suzanne Dale Ezell

Nothing we do is more powerful or more life-changing than praising God.

Stormie Omartian

Is anyone happy? Let him sing songs of praise.

James 5:13 NIV

It's our privilege to not only raise our hands in worship but also to combine the visible with the invisible in a rising stream of praise and adoration sent directly to our Father.

Shirley Dobson

Praise opens the window of our hearts, preparing us to walk more closely with God. Prayer raises the window of our spirit, enabling us to listen more clearly to the Father.

Max Lucado

Most of the verses written about praise in God's Word were voiced by people faced with crushing heartaches, injustice, treachery, slander, and scores of other difficult situations.

Joni Eareckson Tada

More Words from God's Word

Enter into His gates with thanksgiving, and into His courts with praise. Be thankful to Him, and bless His name. For the LORD is good; His mercy is everlasting, and His truth endures to all generations.

Psalm 100:4-5 NKJV

Great is the LORD! He is most worthy of praise! His greatness is beyond discovery!

Psalm 145:3 NLT

I will praise the name of God with a song, and will magnify him with thanksgiving.

Psalm 69:30 KJV

Rejoice in the LORD, O you righteous! For praise from the upright is beautiful.

Psalm 33:1 NKJV

My Values for Life

	Check Your Value High	Med.	Low
I make it a habit to praise God many times each day, beginning with my morning devotional . . .	___	___	___
Whether I am experiencing good times or difficult times, I understand the need to praise God . . .	___	___	___
When I praise God, I feel that I am following in the footsteps of His Son . . .	___	___	___

The Value of a Happy Heart

A happy heart is like a continual feast.

Proverbs 15:15 NCV

Cheerfulness is a gift that we give to others and to ourselves. And, as believers who have been saved by a risen Christ, why shouldn't we be cheerful? The answer, of course, is that we have every reason to honor our Savior with joy in our hearts, smiles on our faces, and words of celebration on our lips.

Few things in life are more sad, or, for that matter, more absurd, than the sight of grumpy Christians trudging unhappily through life. Christ promises us lives of abundance and joy if we accept His love and His grace. Yet sometimes, even the most righteous among us are beset by fits of ill temper and frustration. During these moments, we may not feel like turning our thoughts and prayers to Christ, but that's precisely what we should do.

Mrs. Charles E. Cowman, the author of the classic devotional text *Streams in the Desert*, wrote, "Two wings are necessary to lift our souls toward God: prayer and praise. Prayer asks. Praise accepts the answer." That's why we should find the time to lift our concerns to God in prayer and to praise Him for all that He has done.

John Wesley correctly observed, "Sour godliness is the devil's religion." These words remind us that pessimism and doubt are some of the most important tools that Satan uses to achieve his objectives.

Our challenge, of course, is to ensure that Satan cannot use these tools *on us*.

Are you a cheerful Christian? You should be! And what is the best way to attain the joy that is rightfully yours? By giving Christ what is rightfully His: your heart, your soul, and your life.

When I think of God, my heart is so full of joy that the notes leap and dance as they leave my pen; and since God has given me a cheerful heart, I serve him with a cheerful spirit.

Franz Joseph Haydn

Values for Life

Cheer up somebody else. Do you need a little cheering up? If so, find somebody else who needs cheering up, too. Then, do your best to brighten that person's day. When you do, you'll discover that cheering up other people is a wonderful way to cheer yourself up, too!

Timeless Wisdom for Godly Living

The people whom I have seen succeed best in life have always been cheerful and hopeful people who went about their business with a smile on their faces.

Charles Kingsley

If his presence does not cheer you, surely heaven itself would not make you glad; for what is heaven but the full enjoyment of his love?

C. H. Spurgeon

A cheerful look brings joy to the heart, and good news gives health to the bones.

Proverbs 15:30 NIV

Christ can put a spring in your step and a thrill in your heart. Optimism and cheerfulness are products of knowing Christ.

Billy Graham

God is good, and heaven is forever. And if those two facts don't cheer you up, nothing will.

Marie T. Freeman

The greatest honor you can give Almighty God is to live gladly and joyfully because of the knowledge of His love.

Juliana of Norwich

Cheerfulness

More Words from God's Word

A cheerful heart is good medicine, but a crushed spirit dries up the bones.

Proverbs 17:22 NIV

Jacob said, "For what a relief it is to see your friendly smile. It is like seeing the smile of God!"

Genesis 33:10 NLT

Those who are pure in their thinking are happy, because they will be with God.

Matthew 5:8 NCV

But happy are those . . . whose hope is in the LORD their God.

Psalm 146:5 NLT

He who seeks good finds goodwill, but evil comes to him who searches for it.

Proverbs 11:27 NIV

My Values for Life

	Check Your Value		
	High	Med.	Low
For me, it is important to cultivate an attitude of cheerfulness . . .	___	___	___
Because I understand that emotions are contagious, I try my best to associate with cheerful people . . .	___	___	___
I believe that happiness is not a goal. Happiness is the by-product of my right relationship with God . . .	___	___	___

The Power of an Obedient Heart

Whatever you have learned or received or heard from me,
or seen in me—put it into practice.
And the God of peace will be with you.

Philippians 4:9 NIV

Obedience to God is determined not by words but by deeds. Talking about righteousness is easy; living righteously is far more difficult, especially in today's temptation-filled world.

Since God created Adam and Eve, we human beings have been rebelling against our Creator. Why? Because we are unwilling to trust God's Word, and we are unwilling to follow His commandments. God has given us a guidebook for righteous living called the Holy Bible. It contains thorough instructions which, if followed, lead to fulfillment, abundance, and salvation. But, if we choose to ignore God's commandments, the results are as predictable as they are tragic.

In Ephesians 2:10 we read, "For we are His workmanship, created in Christ Jesus for good works" (NKJV). These words are instructive: We are not saved *by* good works but *for* good works. Good works are not the root but, rather, the fruit of our salvation.

When we seek righteousness in our own lives—and when we seek the companionship of those who do likewise—we reap the spiritual rewards that God intends for our lives. When we behave ourselves as godly men and women, we honor God. When we live righteously and according to God's commandments, He blesses us in ways that we cannot fully understand.

Do you seek God's peace and His blessings? Then obey Him. When you're faced with a difficult choice or a powerful temptation, seek God's counsel and trust the counsel He gives. Invite God into your heart and live according to His commandments. When you do, you will be blessed today and tomorrow and forever.

True faith commits us to obedience.

A. W. Tozer

Values for Life

Obedience leads to spiritual growth: Anne Graham Lotz correctly observed, "If you want to discover your spiritual gifts, start obeying God. As you serve Him, you will find that He has given you the gifts that are necessary to follow through in obedience."

Timeless Wisdom for Godly Living

Our obedience does not make God any bigger or better than He already is. Anything God commands of us is so that our joy may be full—the joy of seeing His glory revealed to us and in us!

Beth Moore

Let me tell you—there is no "high" like the elation and joy that come from a sacrificial act of obedience.

Bill Hybels

But if anyone obeys his word, God's love is truly made complete in him. This is how we know we are in him: Whoever claims to live in him must walk as Jesus did.

1 John 2:5-6 NIV

God does not want the forced obedience of slaves. Instead, He covets the voluntary love and obedience of children who love Him for Himself.

Catherine Marshall

Make this day a day of obedience, a day of spiritual joy, and a day of peace. Make this day's work a little part of the work of the Kingdom of my Lord Christ.

John Baillie

More Words from God's Word

By this we know that we love the children of God,
when we love God and keep His commandments.

1 John 5:2 NKJV

Now that you are obedient children of God do not live as you did
in the past. You did not understand, so you did the evil things you wanted.
But be holy in all you do, just as God, the One who called you, is holy.

1 Peter 1:14-15 NCV

We must obey God rather than men.

Acts 5:29 NASB

You shall walk after the LORD your God and fear Him,
and keep His commandments and obey His voice,
and you shall serve Him and hold fast to Him.

Deuteronomy 13:4 NKJV

My Values for Life

	Check Your Value		
	High	Med.	Low
I understand that my obedience to God is a demonstration of the gratitude that I feel in my heart for the blessings I have been given . . .	___	___	___
When I obey God, I feel better about myself . . .	___	___	___
Obedience to God may not always be easy or pleasant, but it is always satisfying . . .	___	___	___

The Disciplined Life

Discipline yourself for the purpose of godliness.

1 Timothy 4:7 NASB

Are you a self-disciplined person? If so, congratulations . . . if not, it's time to think long and hard about your values, your priorities, and your habits.

God's Word makes it clear that He doesn't reward laziness, misbehavior, or apathy. To the contrary, He expects believers (like you) to behave with dignity and discipline.

You live in a world where leisure is glorified and indifference is often glamorized—but God has bigger things in store for you. He did not create you for a life of mediocrity; He created you for far greater things. God has given you a unique assortment of talents and opportunities . . . and He expects you to use them. But beware: it is not always easy to cultivate those talents.

Sometimes, you must invest countless hours (or, in some cases, many years) honing your skills. And that's perfectly okay with God because He understands that self-discipline is a blessing not a burden.

When you pause to consider how much work needs to be done, you'll realize that self-discipline is not simply a proven way to get ahead; it's also an integral part of God's plan for your life. If you genuinely seek to be faithful stewards of your time, your talents, and your resources, you must adopt a disciplined approach to life. Otherwise, your talents may go unused and your resources may be squandered.

So, as you plan for your future, remember this: life's greatest rewards are unlikely to fall into your lap; to the contrary, your greatest accomplishments will probably require lots of work and plenty of self-discipline. And it's up to you to behave accordingly.

As we seek to become disciples of Jesus Christ,
we should never forget that the word *disciple*
is directly related to the word *discipline*.
To be a disciple of the Lord Jesus Christ is to know his discipline.

Dennis Swanberg

Values for Life

A disciplined lifestyle gives you more control: The more disciplined you become, the more you can take control over your life (which, by the way, is far better than letting your life take control over you).

Timeless Wisdom for Godly Living

Discipline is the refining fire by which talent becomes ability.

Roy L. Smith

So prepare your minds for service and have self-control.

1 Peter 1:13 NCV

Simply stated, self-discipline is obedience to God's Word and willingness to submit everything in life to His will, for His ultimate glory.

John MacArthur

A spiritual life without discipline is impossible. Discipline is the other side of discipleship. The practice of a spiritual discipline makes us more sensitive to the small, gentle voice of God.

Henri Nouwen

The effective Christians of history have been men and women of great personal discipline—mental discipline, discipline of the body, discipline of the tongue, and discipline of the emotion.

Billy Graham

The alternative to discipline is disaster.

Vance Havner

More Words from God's Word

But I discipline my body and bring it into subjection, lest, when I have preached to others, I myself should become disqualified.

1 Corinthians 9:27 NKJV

So prepare your minds for service and have self-control.

1 Peter 1:13 NCV

So don't lose a minute in building on what you've been given, complementing your basic faith with good character, spiritual understanding, alert discipline, passionate patience, reverent wonder, warm friendliness, and generous love, each dimension fitting into and developing the others.

2 Peter 1:5-7 MSG

The fear of the LORD is the beginning of knowledge, but fools despise wisdom and discipline.

Proverbs 1:7 NIV

My Values for Life

	Check Your Value		
	High	Med.	Low
I value the rewards of a disciplined lifestyle . . .	___	___	___
I understand the importance of disciplining myself emotionally, mentally, spiritually, and physically . . .	___	___	___
I believe that when I work hard, my hard work is usually rewarded . . .	___	___	___

Valuing God's Word

Thy word is a lamp unto my feet, and a light unto my path.

Psalm 119:105 KJV

Are you a person who trusts God's Word without reservation? Hopefully so, because the Bible is unlike any other book—it is a guidebook for life here on earth and for life eternal.

As you establish priorities for life, you must decide whether God's Word will be a bright spotlight that guides your path every day or a tiny nightlight that occasionally flickers in the dark. The decision to study the Bible—or not—is yours and yours alone. But make no mistake: how you choose to use your Bible will have a profound impact on you and your loved ones.

As a Christian, you are instructed to study God's Holy Word, to trust His Word, to follow its commandments, and to share its Good News with the world. The Psalmist writes, "Your word is a lamp to my feet and a light to my path" (Psalm 119:105 NASB). Is the Bible your lamp? If not, you are depriving yourself of a priceless gift from the Creator.

Because you are a spiritual being, you have the potential to grow in your personal knowledge of the Lord every day that you live. You can do so through prayer, through worship, through an openness to God's Holy Spirit, and through a careful study of God's Holy Word. Your Bible contains powerful prescriptions for everyday living. If you sincerely seek to walk with God, you should commit yourself to the thoughtful study of His teachings.

Vance Havner observed, "It takes calm, thoughtful, prayerful meditation on the Word to extract its deepest nourishment." How true. God's Word can be a roadmap to a place of righteous and abundance. Make it your roadmap. God's wisdom can be a light to guide your steps. Claim it as your light today, tomorrow, and every day of your life—and then walk confidently in the footsteps of God's only begotten Son.

God has given us all sorts of counsel and direction
in His written Word;
thank God, we have it written down in black and white.

John Eldredge

Values for Life

Trust God's Word: Charles Swindoll writes, "There are four words I wish we would never forget, and they are, 'God keeps his word.'" And remember this: When it comes to studying God's Word, school is always in session.

Timeless Wisdom for Godly Living

God can see clearly no matter how dark or foggy the night is.
Trust His Word to guide you safely home.

Lisa Whelchel

One of the greatest ways God changes me is by bringing Scripture to mind that I have hidden deep in my heart.
And, He always picks the right Scripture at the right time.

Evelyn Christianson

The promises of Scripture are not mere pious hopes or sanctified guesses. They are more than sentimental words to be printed on decorated cards for Sunday School children. They are eternal verities. They are true. There is no perhaps about them.

Peter Marshall

All Scripture is given by inspiration of God, and is profitable for doctrine, for reproof, for correction, for instruction in righteousness.

2 Timothy 3:16 KJV

Prayer and the Word are inseparably linked together.
Power in the use of either depends on the presence of the other.

Andrew Murray

More Words from God's Word

For the word of God is living and effective and sharper than any two-edged sword, penetrating as far as to divide soul, spirit, joints, and marrow; it is a judge of the ideas and thoughts of the heart.

Hebrews 4:12 HCSB

Heaven and earth will pass away, but my words will never pass away.

Matthew 24:35 NIV

Man shall not live by bread alone, but by every word that proceeds from the mouth of God.

Matthew 4:4 NKJV

So then faith comes by hearing, and hearing by the word of God.

Romans 10:17 NKJV

My Values for Life

	Check Your Value		
	High	Med.	Low
I value the Bible as God's word, and I believe that the Bible is true . . .	___	___	___
When my behavior is inconsistent with God's Word, I understand the need to change my behavior . . .	___	___	___
I have a regular time when I study the Bible and meditate upon its meaning for my life . . .	___	___	___

In a World Filled with Temptations . . .

Be careful! Watch out for attacks from the Devil, your great enemy. He prowls around like a roaring lion, looking for some victim to devour. Take a firm stand against him, and be strong in your faith.

1 Peter 5:8-9 NLT

Because our world is filled with temptations, we confront them at every turn. Some of these temptations are small—eating a second bowl of ice cream, for example. Too many desserts may cause us to defile, at least in a modest way, the bodily temple that God has entrusted to our care. But a few extra scoops of ice cream won't bring us to our knees. Other temptations, however, are not so harmless.

The devil, it seems, is working overtime these days, and causing heartache in more places and in more ways than ever before. We, as Christians, must remain vigilant. Not only must we resist Satan when he confronts us, but we must also avoid those places where Satan can most easily tempt us. And, if we are to avoid the unending temptations of this world, we must arm ourselves with the Word of God.

In a letter to believers, Peter offered a stern warning: "Be sober, be vigilant; because your adversary the devil walks about like a roaring lion, seeking whom he may devour" (1 Peter 5:8 NKJV). What was true in New Testament times is equally true in our own. Satan tempts his prey and then devours them. And in these dangerous times, the tools that Satan uses to destroy his prey are more numerous than ever before.

As believing Christians, we must beware. And, if we seek righteousness in our own lives, we must earnestly wrap ourselves in the protection of God's Holy Word. After fasting forty days and nights in the desert, Jesus Himself was tempted by Satan. Christ used Scripture to rebuke the devil (Matthew 4:1-11). We must do likewise. The Holy Bible provides us with a perfect blueprint for righteous living. If we consult that blueprint daily and follow it carefully, we build our lives according to God's plan. And when we do, we are secure.

Do not fight the temptation in detail.
Turn from it. Look only at your Lord. Sing. Read. Work.

Amy Carmichael

Values for Life

You live in a "Temptation Nation": At every turn in the road, or so it seems, somebody is trying to tempt you with something. Your job is to steer clear of temptation . . . and to keep steering clear as long as you live. Remember the old saying: "When it comes to temptation, it's easier to stay out than it is to get out."

Timeless Wisdom for Godly Living

The Bible teaches us in times of temptation there is one command:
Flee! Get away from it, for every struggle against lust
using only one's own strength is doomed to failure.

Dietrich Bonhoeffer

But remember that the temptations that come into your life are no different from what others experience. And God is faithful. He will keep the temptation from becoming so strong that you can't stand up against it. When you are tempted, he will show you a way out so that you will not give in to it.

1 Corinthians 10:13 NLT

Some temptations come to the industrious,
but all temptations attack the idle.

C. H. *Spurgeon*

The higher the hill, the stronger the wind: so the loftier the life,
the stronger the enemy's temptations.

John Wycliffe

We can't stop the Adversary from whispering in our ears,
but we can refuse to listen, and we can definitely refuse to respond.

Liz Curtis Higgs

More Words from God's Word

The Lord knows how to deliver the godly out of temptations.

2 Peter 2:9 NKJV

Put on the whole armour of God, that ye may be able to stand against the wiles of the devil.

Ephesians 6:11 KJV

Blessed is the man who endures temptation; for when he has been approved, he will receive the crown of life which the Lord has promised to those who love Him.

James 1:12 NKJV

Yet in all these things we are more than conquerors through Him who loved us.

Romans 8:37 NKJV

My Values for Life

	Check Your Value		
	High	Med.	Low
I trust that God can help me overcome any temptation . . .	___	___	___
When faced with temptation, I turn my thoughts and my prayers to God . . .	___	___	___
I try to avoid situations where I might be tempted . . .	___	___	___

A Lifetime of Spiritual Growth

But grow in the grace and knowledge of our Lord and Savior Jesus Christ. To Him be the glory both now and forever.

2 Peter 3:18 NKJV

The path to spiritual maturity unfolds day by day. Each day offers the opportunity to worship God, to ignore God, or to rebel against God. When we worship Him with our prayers, our words, our thoughts, and our actions, we are blessed by the richness of our relationship with the Father. But if we ignore God altogether or intentionally rebel against His commandments, we rob ourselves of His blessings.

If we study God's Word, if we obey His commandments, and if we live in the center of His will, we will not be "stagnant" believers; we will, instead, be growing Christians . . . and that's exactly what God wants for our lives.

Many of life's most important lessons are painful to learn, but spiritual growth need not take place only in times of adversity. We must seek to grow in our knowledge and love of the Lord in every season of life. Thankfully, God always stands at the door; whenever we are ready to reach out to Him, He will answer.

In those quiet moments when we open our hearts to the Father, the One who made us keeps remaking us. He gives us direction, perspective, wisdom, and courage. And, the appropriate moment to accept those spiritual gifts is always the present one.

Are you as mature as you're ever going to be? Hopefully not! When it comes to your faith, God doesn't intend for you to become "fully grown," at least not in this lifetime. In fact, God still has important lessons that He intends to teach you. So ask yourself this: what lesson is God trying to teach me today? And then go about the business of learning it.

We have tasted "that the LORD is good" (Psalm 34:8),
but we don't yet know how good he is.
We only know that his sweetness makes us long for more.

C. H. *Spurgeon*

Values for Life

Change is inevitable; growth is not: The world keeps changing, and so, hopefully, do we. We are mightily tempted to remain stagnant (we perceive that it's safer "here" than "there"). But God has bigger plans for us. He intends that we continue to mature throughout every stage of life. Toward that end, God comes to our doorsteps with countless opportunities to learn and to grow. And He knocks. Our challenge, of course, is to open the door.

Timeless Wisdom for Godly Living

I've never met anyone who became instantly mature. It's a painstaking process that God takes us through, and it includes such things as waiting, failing, losing, and being misunderstood—each calling for extra doses of perseverance.

Charles Swindoll

Long for the pure milk of the word, so that by it you may grow in respect to salvation.

1 Peter 2:2 NASB

Growing in any area of the Christian life takes time, and the key is daily sitting at the feet of Jesus.

Cynthia Heald

There is wonderful freedom and joy in coming to recognize that the fun is in the becoming.

Gloria Gaither

I do not know how the Spirit of Christ performs it, but He brings us choices through which we constantly change, fresh and new, into His likeness.

Joni Eareckson Tada

Spiritual Maturity

More Words from God's Word

When I was a child, I spoke and thought and reasoned as a child does. But when I grew up, I put away childish things.

1 Corinthians 13:11 NLT

It was he who gave some to be apostles, some to be prophets, some to be evangelists, and some to be pastors and teachers, to prepare God's people for works of service, so that the body of Christ may be built up until we all reach unity in the faith and in the knowledge of the Son of God and become mature, attaining to the whole measure of the fullness of Christ.

Ephesians 4:11-13 NIV

Therefore let us leave the elementary teachings about Christ and go on to maturity . . . .

Hebrews 6:1 NIV

My Values for Life

	Check Your Value		
	High	Med.	Low
I understand the value of spiritual growth . . .	___	___	___
I believe that spiritual maturity is a journey, not a destination . . .	___	___	___
I believe that regular, consistent study of God's Word ensures that I will continue to grow as a Christian . . .	___	___	___

A Heart Filled with Joy

These things I have spoken to you, that My joy may remain in you, and that your joy may be full.

John 15:11 NKJV

Christ made it clear to His followers: He intended that *His* joy would become *their* joy. And it still holds true today: Christ intends that His believers share His love with His joy in their hearts. Yet sometimes, amid the inevitable hustle and bustle of life here on earth, we can forfeit—albeit temporarily—the joy of Christ as we wrestle with the challenges of daily living.

Happiness depends less upon our circumstances than upon our thoughts. When we turn our thoughts to God, to His gifts, and to His glorious creation, we experience the joy that God intends for His children. But, when we focus on the negative aspects of life, we suffer needlessly.

Psalm 100 reminds us that, as believers, we have every reason to celebrate: "Shout for joy to the LORD, all the earth. Worship the LORD with gladness" (vv. 1-2 NIV). And C. H. Spurgeon, the renowned 19th-century English clergymen, advised, "The Lord is glad to open the gate to every knocking soul. It opens very freely; its hinges are not rusted; no bolts secure it. Have faith and enter at this moment through holy courage. If you knock with a heavy heart, you shall yet sing with joy of spirit. Never be discouraged!"

So today, if your heart is heavy, open the door of your soul to Christ. He will give you peace and joy. And, if you already have the joy of Christ in your heart, share it freely, just as Christ freely shared His joy with you.

Our obedience does not make God any bigger or better than He already is. Anything God commands of us is so that our joy may be full—the joy of seeing His glory revealed to us and in us!

Beth Moore

Values for Life

Joy begins with a choice: the choice to establish a genuine relationship with God and His Son. As Amy Carmichael correctly observed, "Joy is not gush; joy is not mere jolliness. Joy is perfect acquiescence, acceptance, and rest in God's will, whatever comes."

Timeless Wisdom for Godly Living

Joy in life is not the absence of sorrow.
The fact that Jesus could have joy in the midst of sorrow
is proof that we can experience this too.

Warren Wiersbe

Some of us seem so anxious about avoiding hell
that we forget to celebrate our journey toward heaven.

Philip Yancey

A life of intimacy with God is characterized by joy.

Oswald Chambers

Let the hearts of those who seek the LORD rejoice.
Look to the LORD and his strength; seek his face always.

1 Chronicles 16:10-11 NIV

I choose joy. I will refuse the temptation to be cynical;
cynicism is the tool of a lazy thinker. I will refuse to see people
as anything less than human beings, created by God.
I will refuse to see any problem as anything less
than an opportunity to see God.

Max Lucado

The chief end of man is to glorify God and enjoy him forever.

Westminister Shorter Catechism

More Words from God's Word

A joyful heart is good medicine, but a broken spirit dries up the bones.

Proverbs 17:22 NASB

Make a joyful noise unto the LORD*, all ye lands. Serve the* LORD *with gladness: come before his presence with singing.*

Psalm 100:1-2 KJV

This is the day the LORD *has made; let us rejoice and be glad in it.*

Psalm 118:24 NIV

May the God of hope fill you with all joy and peace as you trust in him, so that you may overflow with hope by the power of the Holy Spirit.

Romans 15:13 NIV

My Values for Life

Check Your Value			
	High	Med.	Low
Because I am a Christian, I believe that my joy does not depend upon my circumstances, but on my relationship with God . . .	___	___	___
When I count my blessings and thank God for those blessings, I am more joyful . . .	___	___	___
When I participate in regular heartfelt worship, I am more joyful . . .	___	___	___

The Power of Simplicity

A simple life in the Fear-of-God is better than a rich life with a ton of headaches.

Proverbs 15:16 MSG

You live in a world where simplicity is in short supply. Think for a moment about the complexity of your life and compare it to the lives of your ancestors. Certainly, you are the beneficiary of many technological innovations, but these innovations have a price: in all likelihood, your world is highly complex. Consider the following:

1. From the moment you wake up in the morning until the time you lay your head on the pillow at night, you are the target of an endless stream of advertising information. Each message is intended to grab your attention in order to convince you to purchase things you didn't know you needed (and probably don't!).

2. Essential aspects of your life, including personal matters such as health care, are subject to an ever-increasing flood of rules and regulations.

3. Unless you take firm control of your time and your life, you may be overwhelmed by a tidal wave of complexity that threatens your happiness.

Is yours a life of moderation or accumulation? Are you more interested in the possessions you can acquire or in the person you can become? The answers to these questions will determine the direction of your day and, in time, the direction of your life.

If your material possessions are somehow distancing you from God, discard them. If your outside interests leave you too little time for your family or your Creator, slow down the merry-go-round, or better yet, get off the merry-go-round completely. Remember: God wants your full attention, and He wants it today, so don't let anybody or anything get in His way.

The most powerful life is the most simple life.
The most powerful life is the life that knows where it's going,
that knows where the source of strength is;
it is the life that stays free of clutter and
happenstance and hurriedness.

Max Lucado

Values for Life

Simplicity is beautiful: If your mailbox is overflowing with credit card bills and your bank balance is approaching single digits, it's officially time to simplify your life. But before you unload that seldom-used food processor at your next yard sale, toss your credit cards into the blender and push "Liquefy."

Timeless Wisdom for Godly Living

There is absolutely no evidence that complexity and materialism lead to happiness. On the contrary, there is plenty of evidence that simplicity and spirituality lead to joy, a blessedness that is better than happiness.

Dennis Swanberg

Prescription for a happier and healthier life: resolve to slow down your pace; learn to say no gracefully; resist the temptation to chase after more pleasure, more hobbies, and more social entanglements.

James Dobson

We brought nothing into the world, so we can take nothing out. But, if we have food and clothes, we will be satisfied with that.

1 Timothy 6:7-8 NCV

In the name of Jesus Christ who was never in a hurry, we pray, O God, that You will slow us down, for we know that we live too fast. With all eternity before us, make us take time to live—time to get acquainted with You, time to enjoy Your blessing, and time to know each other.

Peter Marshall

More Words from God's Word

He that giveth, let him do it with simplicity . . . .

Romans 12:8 KJV

The L*ORD preserves the simple; when I was brought low, he saved me.*

Psalm 116:6 RSV

As newborn babies want milk, you should want the pure and simple teaching. By it you can grow up and be saved.

1 Peter 2:2 NCV

The law of the L*ORD is perfect, converting the soul: the testimony of the* L*ORD is sure, making wise the simple.*

Psalm 19:7 KJV

My Values for Life

	Check Your Value		
	High	Med.	Low
I value the benefits of simplicity . . .	___	___	___
The world leads me toward a life of complexity and stress. God leads me toward simplicity and peace . . .	___	___	___
I understand that the accumulation of material possessions does not ensure a joyful life; it is my relationship with God (and my obedience to Him) that brings me abundance and joy . . .	___	___	___

The Value of Faith

Have faith in the LORD your God and you will be upheld; have faith in his prophets and you will be successful.

2 Chronicles 20:20 NIV

When a suffering woman sought healing by merely touching the hem of His cloak, Jesus replied, "Daughter, be of good comfort; thy faith hath made thee whole" (Matthew 9:22 KJV). Christ's message is clear: we should live by faith. But, when we face adversity, illness, or heartbreak, living by faith can be difficult indeed. Yet this much is certain: whatever our circumstances, we must continue to plant the seeds of faith in our hearts, trusting that in time God will bring forth a bountiful harvest.

Have you, on occasion, felt your faith in God slipping away? If so, consider yourself a member of a very large club. We human beings are subject to an assortment of negative emotions such as fear, worry, anxiety, and doubt. When we fall short of perfect faith, God understands us and forgives us. And, God stands ready to strengthen us *if* we turn our doubts and fears over to Him.

As you enter into the next phase of your life, you'll face many experiences: some good, and some not so good. When the sun is shining and all is well, it is easier to have faith. But, when life takes an unexpected turn for the worse, as it will from time to time, your faith will be tested. In times of trouble and doubt, God remains faithful to you. Do the same for Him.

Are you tapped in to the power of faith? Hopefully so. The hours that you invest in Bible study, prayer, meditation, and worship should be times of enrichment and celebration. And, if your faith is being tested to the point of breaking, know that your Savior is near. Reach out to Him, and let Him heal your broken spirit. Be content to touch even the smallest fragment of the Master's garment, and He will make you whole.

This life of faith, then, consists in just this—being a child in the Father's house. Let the ways of childish confidence and freedom from care, which so please you and win your heart when you observe your own little ones, teach you what you should be in your attitude toward God.

Hannah Whitall Smith

Values for Life

Faith should be practiced more than studied. Vance Havner said, "Nothing is more disastrous than to study faith, analyze faith, make noble resolves of faith, but never actually to make the leap of faith." How true!

Timeless Wisdom for Godly Living

When you and I place our faith in Jesus Christ and invite Him
to come live within us, the Holy Spirit comes upon us,
and the power of God overshadows us,
and the life of Jesus is born within us.

Anne Graham Lotz

Seldom do you enjoy the luxury of making decisions
that are based on enough evidence to absolutely silence all skepticism.

Bill Hybels

Fight the good fight of faith;
take hold of the eternal life to which you were called . . . .

1 Timothy 6:12 NASB

Those who make religion consist altogether in good works overlook
the fact that works themselves are not acceptable to God unless they
proceed from faith. For without faith, it is impossible to please Him.
And those who make religion consist altogether in faith overlook
the fact that true faith always works by love,
and invariably produces the works of love.

Charles Finney

Faith is not merely you holding on to God—
it is God holding on to you.

E. Stanley Jones

More Words from God's Word

We live by faith, not by sight.

2 Corinthians 5:7 NIV

*Let us come near to God with a sincere heart and a sure faith,
because we have been made free from a guilty conscience,
and our bodies have been washed with pure water.*

Hebrews 10:22 NCV

*The fundamental fact of existence is that this trust in God, this faith,
is the firm foundation under everything that makes life worth living.*

Hebrews 11:1 MSG

*Let us run with endurance the race that is set before us,
fixing our eyes on Jesus, the author and perfecter of faith.*

Hebrews 12:1-2 NASB

Faith without works is dead.

James 2:20 KJV

My Values for Life

	Check Your Value		
	High	Med.	Low
I believe in the power of faith to "make me whole" . . .	___	___	___
My faith is stronger when I keep my eyes on Jesus and not on my circumstances . . .	___	___	___
I believe that faith is a choice, and I choose to have faith . . .	___	___	___

The Right Kind of Example

Be an example to the believers in word, in conduct, in love, in spirit, in faith, in purity.

1 Timothy 4:12 NKJV

Whether we like it or not, all of us are role models. Our friends and family members watch our actions and, as followers of Christ, we are obliged to act accordingly.

What kind of example are you? Are you the kind of person whose life serves as a genuine example of righteousness? Does your behavior serve as a positive role model for others? Are you the kind of believer whose actions, day in and day out, are based upon kindness, faithfulness, and a love for the Lord? If so, you are not only blessed by God, but you are also a powerful force for good in a world that desperately needs positive influences such as yours.

Phillips Brooks had simple advice for believers of every generation; he said, "Be such a person, and live such a life, that if every person were such as you, and every life a life like yours, this earth would be God's Paradise." And that's precisely the kind of Christian you should strive to be . . . but it isn't always easy.

You live in a dangerous, temptation-filled world. That's why you encounter so many opportunities to stray from God's commandments. Resist those temptations! When you do, you'll earn

God's blessings, and you'll serve as a positive role model for your family and friends.

Corrie ten Boom advised, "Don't worry about what you do not understand. Worry about what you do understand in the Bible but do not live by." And that's sound advice because your families and friends are watching . . . and so, for that matter, is God.

Be careful how you live.
You may be the only Bible some person ever reads.

William J. Toms

Values for Life

Your life is a sermon . . . What kind of sermon will you preach? The words you choose to speak may have some impact on others, but not nearly as much impact as the life you choose to live.

Timeless Wisdom for Godly Living

Preach the gospel every day; if necessary, use words.

St. Francis of Assisi

If you want your neighbor to know what Christ will do for him,
let the neighbor see what Christ has done for you.

Henry Ward Beecher

I'd rather see a sermon than hear one any day;
I'd rather one should walk with me than merely tell the way.

Edgar A. Guest

You are the light that gives light to the world . . . .
In the same way, you should be a light for other people.
Live so that they will see the good things you do
and will praise your Father in heaven.

Matthew 5:14,16 NCV

There is a transcendent power in example.
We reform others unconsciously when we walk uprightly.

Anne Sophie Swetchine

More Words from God's Word

We have around us many people whose lives tell us what faith means. So let us run the race that is before us and never give up. We should remove from our lives anything that would get in the way and the sin that so easily holds us back.

Hebrews 12:1 NCV

I have set you an example that you should do as I have done for you.

John 13:15 NIV

As an example, brethren, of suffering and patience, take the prophets who spoke in the name of the LORD. Behold we count those blessed who endured. You have heard of the endurance of Job and have seen the outcome of the LORD's dealings, that the LORD is full of compassion and is merciful.

James 5:10-11 NASB

My Values for Life

	Check Your Value		
	High	Med.	Low
I value the importance of setting a good example . . .	___	___	___
I understand that my behavior speaks volumes about my relationship with God . . .	___	___	___
I understand that I am a role model to my family and friends, and I behave accordingly . . .	___	___	___

A Willingness to Serve

The greatest among you will be your servant.
Whoever exalts himself will be humbled,
and whoever humbles himself will be exalted.

Matthew 23:11-12 HCSB

We live in a world that glorifies power, prestige, fame, and money. But the words of Jesus teach us that the most esteemed men and women are not the widely acclaimed leaders of society; the most esteemed among us are the humble servants of society.

When we experience success, it's easy to puff out our chests and proclaim, "I did that!" But it's wrong. Whatever "it" is, God did it, and He deserves the credit. As Christians, we have been refashioned and saved by Jesus Christ, and that salvation came not because of our own good works but because of God's grace.

Dietrich Bonhoeffer was correct when he observed, "It is very easy to overestimate the importance of our own achievements in comparison with what we owe others." In other words, reality breeds humility.

Are you willing to become a humble servant for Christ? Are you willing to pitch in and make the world a better place, or are you determined to keep all your blessings to yourself? The answer to these questions will determine the quantity and the quality of the service you render to God—and to His children.

Today, you may feel the temptation to take more than you give. You may be tempted to withhold your generosity. Or you may be tempted to build yourself up in the eyes of your friends. Resist these temptations. Instead, serve your friends quietly and without fanfare. Find a need and fill it . . . humbly. Lend a helping hand . . . anonymously. Share a word of kindness . . . with quiet sincerity. As you go about your daily activities, remember that the Savior of all humanity made Himself a servant, and you, as His follower, must do no less.

Christianity, in its purest form, is nothing more than seeing Jesus. Christian service, in its purest form, is nothing more than imitating him whom we see. To see his Majesty and to imitate him: that is the sum of Christianity.

Max Lucado

Values for Life

Whatever your age, whatever your circumstances, you can serve: Each stage of life's journey is a glorious opportunity to place yourself in the service of the One who is the Giver of all blessings. As long as you live, you should honor God with your service to others.

Timeless Wisdom for Godly Living

God does not do anything with us, only through us.

Oswald Chambers

If anyone serves Me, let him follow Me;
and where I am, there My servant will be also.
If anyone serves Me, him My Father will honor.

John 12:26 NKJV

Service is love in overalls!

Anonymous

If you aren't serving, you're just existing,
because life is meant for ministry.

Rick Warren

Without God, we cannot. Without us, God will not.

St. Augustine

As Jesus repeatedly declared, the path to greatness in the kingdom follows the route he himself pioneered, self-sacrificial service to others. As a result, the prominent persons in God's new order will be those who are servants of all.

Stanley Grenz

More Words from God's Word

Think of yourselves the way Christ Jesus thought of himself. He had equal status with God but didn't think so much of himself that he had to cling to the advantages of that status no matter what. Not at all. When the time came, he set aside the privileges of deity and took on the status of a slave, became human! Having become human, he stayed human. It was an incredibly humbling process. He didn't claim special privileges. Instead he lived a selfless, obedient life and then died a selfless, obedient death, and the worst kind of death at that: a crucifixion.

Philippians 2:5-8 MSG

Therefore, since we receive a kingdom which cannot be shaken, let us show gratitude, by which we may offer to God an acceptable service with reverence and awe . . . .

Hebrews 12:28 NASB

There are different kinds of gifts, but they are all from the same Spirit. There are different ways to serve but the same Lord to serve.

1 Corinthians 12:4-5 NCV

My Values for Life

	Check Your Value		
	High	Med.	Low
Christ was a humble servant, and I value the importance of following His example . . .	___	___	___
Greatness in God's kingdom relates to service, not status . . .	___	___	___
I am proactive in my search to find ways to help others . . .	___	___	___

Too Busy for Our Own Good

Discretion is a life-giving fountain to those who possess it . . . .

Proverbs 16:22 NLT

Has the busy pace of life robbed you of the peace that might otherwise be yours through Jesus Christ? If so, you are simply too busy for your own good. Jesus offers you a peace that passes human understanding, but He won't force His peace upon you; in order to experience it, you must slow down long enough to sense His presence and His love.

As a busy person, you may have difficulty investing large blocks of time in much-needed thought and self-reflection. If so, it may be time to reorder your priorities and your values.

God has big plans for you. Discovering those plans will require trial and error, meditation and prayer, faith and perseverance. The moments that you spend with God will help you gather your thoughts and plan for the future. And the time that you spend discussing your dreams with friends and mentors can be invaluable. But, no one can force you to carve out time for life's meaningful moments; it's up to you.

Each waking moment holds the potential to think a creative thought or offer a heartfelt prayer. So even if you're a person with too many demands and too few hours in which to meet them, don't panic. Instead, be comforted in the knowledge that when you sincerely seek to discover God's purpose for your life, He will respond in marvelous and surprising ways. Remember: this is the day that He has made, and He has filled it with countless opportunities to love, to serve, and to seek His guidance. Seize those opportunities today, and keep seizing them every day that you live.

Often our lives are strangled by things that don't ultimately matter.

Grady Nutt

Values for Life

Daily devotionals never go out of style: are you too busy to lead a daily devotional with your family? If so, it's time to reorder your priorities.

Timeless Wisdom for Godly Living

Being busy, in and of itself, is not a sin. But being busy in an endless pursuit of things that leave us empty and hollow and broken inside—that cannot be pleasing to God.

Max Lucado

Then the apostles gathered to Jesus and told Him all things, both what they had done and what they had taught. And He said to them, "Come aside by yourselves to a deserted place and rest a while." For there were many coming and going, and they did not even have time to eat.

Mark 6:30-31 NKJV

Noise and words and frenzied, hectic schedules dull our senses, closing our ears to His still, small voice and making us numb to His touch.

Charles Swindoll

This is a day when we are so busy doing everything that we have no time to be anything. Even religiously we are so occupied with activities that we have no time to know God.

Vance Havner

There is an enormous power in little things to distract our attention from God.

Oswald Chambers

More Words from God's Word

Now it happened as they went that He entered a certain village; and a certain woman named Martha welcomed Him into her house. And she had a sister called Mary, who also sat at Jesus' feet and heard His word. But Martha was distracted with much serving, and she approached Him and said, "Lord, do You not care that my sister has left me to serve alone? Therefore tell her to help me." And Jesus answered and said to her, "Martha, Martha, you are worried and troubled about many things. But one thing is needed, and Mary has chosen that good part, which will not be taken away from her."

Luke 10:38-42 NKJV

So teach us to number our days, that we may gain a heart of wisdom.

Psalm 90:12 NKJV

Be still, and know that I am God.

Psalm 46:10 NKJV

My Values for Life

	Check Your Value		
	High	Med.	Low
I understand the importance of setting priorities . . .	___	___	___
After I have established priorities for the coming day, I value the importance of doing first things first . . .	___	___	___
Because I understand that I cannot do everything, I understand the importance of saying no when it's appropriate to do so . . .	___	___	___

Balance

On Beyond Failure

For though a righteous man falls seven times, he rises again . . . .

Proverbs 24:16 NIV

From time to time, all of us face life-altering disappointments that leave us breathless. Oftentimes, these disappointments come unexpectedly, leaving us with more questions than answers. But even when we don't have all the answers, God does. Whatever our circumstances, whether we stand atop the highest mountain or wander through the darkest valley, God is ready to protect us, to comfort us, and to heal us. Our task is to let Him.

Life is a tapestry of events: some grand, some not-so-grand, some disappointing, and some tragic. During the happy times, we are tempted to take our blessings for granted (a temptation that we must resist with all our might). But, during life's difficult days, we discover precisely what we're made of. And more importantly, we discover what our faith is made of.

If your faith is being tested by difficult circumstances, here are some things to consider:

Your Response: God wants you to respond to life's disappointing moments with an attitude of obedience. No matter how difficult your circumstances, God calls you to obey the instructions that are contained in His Holy Word. He wants you to remain hopeful (Psalm 31:24); He instructs you to remain faithful to Him, and He wants you to be courageous (Matthew 8:26). God also expects you to forgive those who have injured you (Matthew 6:14-15), and He wants you to treat others with kindness and gentleness (Ephesians 4:32). These commandments are often difficult to obey—especially when you feel angry or hurt—but obey them you must . . . otherwise you invite God's disapproval.

Your Lessons: What does God want you to learn from your disappointments? Plenty! Every disappointing chapter of life has important lessons to teach, but no one can learn those lessons for you—you must learn them for yourself. And with God's help, you will.

Your Future: If you've endured a life-altering disappointment, you may have good reason to ask, "Where do you want me to go from here, Lord?" And you may rest assured that, in time, your Heavenly Father will answer you. His answer may not come immediately, and it may not come in a way that you expect, but of this you can be certain: if you sincerely ask, God will answer (Matthew 7:7-8).

When tough times arrive, you should learn from your experiences, and you should prayerfully seek God's guidance for the future. Then, you should tackle the work at hand—the difficult and rewarding work of overcoming your disappointments. When you do your part, you can be certain that God will do His part. And you can be sure that in time, your loving Heavenly Father will turn your stumbling blocks into stepping stones.

Values for Life

Failure isn't permanent . . . unless you fail to bounce back. So pick yourself up, dust yourself off, and trust God. He will make it right. Warren Wiersbe had this advice: "No matter how badly we have failed, we can always get up and begin again. Our God is the God of new beginnings." And don't forget: the best time to begin again is now.

Timeless Wisdom for Godly Living

Why should I ever resist any delay or disappointment, any affliction or oppression or humiliation, when I know God will use it in my life to make me like Jesus and to prepare me for heaven?

Kay Arthur

The next time you're disappointed, don't panic and don't give up. Just be patient and let God remind you he's still in control.

Max Lucado

But as for you, be strong and do not give up, for your work will be rewarded.

2 Chronicles 15:7 NIV

The amazing thing is that God follows us into the blackened ruins of our failed dreams, our misbegotten mirages, into the house of cards that has collapsed on us in some way, and he speaks, not with the chastisement we feel we deserve, but of all things, with tenderness.

Paula Rinehart

Recently I've been learning that life comes down to this: God is in everything. Regardless of what difficulties I am experiencing at the moment, or what things aren't as I would like them to be, I look at the circumstances and say, "Lord, what are you trying to teach me?"

Catherine Marshall

More Words from God's Word

Let us not become weary in doing good,
for at the proper time we will reap a harvest if we do not give up.

Galatians 6:9 NIV

You need to persevere so that when you have done the will of God,
you will receive what he has promised.

Hebrews 10:36 NIV

Be of good courage, and he shall strengthen your heart,
all ye that hope in the LORD.

Psalm 31:24 KJV

Unto thee, O my strength, will I sing:
for God is my defense, and the God of my mercy.

Psalm 59:17 KJV

My Values for Life

	Check Your Value		
	High	Med.	Low
I value the need to keep my disappointments in perspective . . .	___	___	___
I believe that adversity can be a stepping stone to success.	___	___	___
I believe that I have much to learn from adversity . . .	___	___	___

The Value of Enthusiasm

Do your work with enthusiasm.
Work as if you were serving the LORD,
not as if you were serving only men and women.

Ephesians 6:7 NCV

Can you honestly say that you are an enthusiastic believer? Are you passionate about your faith and excited about your path? Hopefully so. But if your zest for life has waned, it is now time to redirect your efforts and recharge your spiritual batteries. And that means refocusing your values by putting God first.

Nothing is more important than your wholehearted commitment to your Creator and to His only begotten Son. Your faith must never be an afterthought; it must be your ultimate priority, your ultimate possession, and your ultimate passion. When you become passionate about your faith, you will become passionate about your life, too.

Norman Vincent Peale advised, "Get absolutely enthralled with something. Throw yourself into it with abandon. Get out of yourself. Be somebody. Do something." His words still ring true. But sometimes, when the stresses of everyday life seem overwhelming, you may not feel very enthusiastic about your life or yourself. If so, it's time to reorder your thoughts, your priorities, your values, and your prayers. When you do, you'll be helping yourself, but you'll also be helping your family and friends.

Genuine, heartfelt, enthusiastic Christianity is contagious. If you enjoy a life-altering relationship with God, that relationship will have an impact on others—perhaps a profound impact.

Are you genuinely excited about your faith? And do you make your enthusiasm known to those around you? Or are you satisfied to be a "silent ambassador" for Christ? God's preference is clear: He intends that you stand before others and proclaim your faith.

Remember: You are the recipient of Christ's sacrificial love. Accept it enthusiastically and share it passionately. Jesus deserves your enthusiasm; the world deserves it; and you deserve the experience of sharing it.

One of the great needs in the church today is for every Christian to become enthusiastic about his faith in Jesus Christ.

Billy Graham

Values for Life

Don't wait for enthusiasm to find you . . . go looking for it. Look at your life and your relationships as exciting adventures. Don't wait for life to spice itself; spice things up yourself.

Timeless Wisdom for Godly Living

We act as though comfort and luxury were the chief requirements of life, when all we need to make us really happy is something to be enthusiastic about.

Charles Kingsley

Don't take hold of a thing unless you want that thing to take hold of you.

E. Stanley Jones

Whatever you do, work at it with all your heart, as working for the LORD, not for men.

Colossians 3:23 NIV

Wherever you are, be all there. Live to the hilt every situation you believe to be the will of God.

Jim Elliot

Diligence applies to whatever you do in your Christian life. Anything done in the Lord's service is worth doing with enthusiasm and care.

John MacArthur

More Words from God's Word

Do not lack diligence; be fervent in spirit; serve the Lord.

Romans 12:11 HCSB

He did it with all his heart. So he prospered.

2 Chronicles 31:21 NKJV

O clap your hands, all peoples; Shout to God with the voice of joy.

Psalm 47:1 NASB

Don't look for shortcuts to God. The market is flooded with surefire, easygoing formulas for a successful life that can be practiced in your spare time. Don't fall for that stuff, even though crowds of people do. The way to life—to God!—is vigorous and requires total attention.

Matthew 7:13-14 MSG

My Values for Life

	Check Your Value		
	High	Med.	Low
My faith gives me reason to be enthusiastic about life . . .	___	___	___
For me, it is important to generate enthusiastic thoughts . . .	___	___	___
When I praise God and thank Him for His blessings, I feel enthusiastic about life . . .	___	___	___

A Lifetime of Learning

Whoever listens to what is taught will succeed,
and whoever trusts the LORD will be happy.

Proverbs 16:20 NCV

Whether you're twenty-two or a hundred and two, you've still got lots to learn. Even if you're very wise, God isn't finished with you yet, and He isn't finished teaching you important lessons about life here on earth and life eternal.

God does not intend for you to be a stagnant believer. Far from it! God wants you to continue growing as a person and as a Christian every day that you live. And make no mistake: both spiritual and intellectual growth are possible during every stage of life.

Are you a curious Christian who has committed yourself to the regimen of regular Bible study, or do you consult your Bible on a hit-or-miss basis? The answer to this question will be an indication of the extent to which you allow God to direct the course of your life.

As a spiritual being, you have the potential to grow in your personal knowledge of the Lord every day that you live. You can do so through prayer, through worship, through an openness to God's Holy Spirit, and through a careful study of God's Holy Word. Your Bible contains powerful prescriptions for everyday living. If you sincerely seek to walk with God, you should commit yourself to the thoughtful study of His teachings.

Do you seek to live a life of righteousness and wisdom? If so, you must continue to study the ultimate source of wisdom: the Word of God. You must associate, day in and day out, with godly men and women. And, you must act in accordance with your beliefs.

When you study God's Word and live according to His commandments, you will become wise . . . and you will serve as a shining example to your friends, to your family, and to the world.

The wonderful thing about God's schoolroom is that we get
to grade our own papers. You see, He doesn't test us
so He can learn how well we're doing.
He tests us so *we* can discover how well we're doing.

Charles Swindoll

Values for Life

Stress the importance of learning: Some families stress the importance of education more than other families. Make yours a home in which the importance of lifetime learning is clearly a high priority.

Timeless Wisdom for Godly Living

Today is yesterday's pupil.

Thomas Fuller

A wise man will hear and increase in learning, and a man of understanding will acquire wise counsel.

Proverbs 1:5 NASB

The wise man gives proper appreciation in his life to his past. He learns to sift the sawdust of heritage in order to find the nuggets that make the current moment have any meaning.

Grady Nutt

The doorstep to the temple of wisdom is a knowledge of our own ignorance.

C. H. *Spurgeon*

Knowledge is power.

Francis Bacon

It's the things you learn after you know it all that really count.

Vance Havner

More Words from God's Word

The knowledge of the secrets of the kingdom of heaven has been given to you . . . .

Matthew 13:11 NIV

For this very reason, make every effort to supplement your faith with goodness, goodness with knowledge, knowledge with self-control, self-control with endurance, endurance with godliness.

2 Peter 1:5-6 HCSB

The fear of the LORD is the beginning of knowledge, but fools despise wisdom and discipline.

Proverbs 1:7 NIV

By wisdom a house is built, and through understanding it is established; through knowledge its rooms are filled with rare and beautiful treasures.

Proverbs 24:3-4 NIV

My Values for Life

	Check Your Value		
	High	Med.	Low
I value the importance of lifetime learning . . .	___	___	___
God's wisdom sometimes opposes the world's wisdom; I choose God's wisdom . . .	___	___	___
I can learn from the past, but I don't choose to live in the past . . .	___	___	___

The Value of Encouragement

But encourage each other daily, while it is still called today, so that none of you is hardened by sin's deception.

Hebrews 3:13 HCSB

Life is a team sport, and all of us need occasional pats on the back from our teammates. This world can be a difficult place, a place where many of our friends and family members are troubled by the challenges of everyday life. And since we cannot always be certain who needs our help, we should strive to speak helpful words to all who cross our paths.

In his letter to the Ephesians, Paul writes, "Do not let any unwholesome talk come out of your mouths, but only what is helpful for building others up according to their needs, that it may benefit those who listen" (4:29 NIV). This passage reminds us that, as Christians, we are instructed to choose our words carefully so as to build others up through wholesome, honest encouragement. How can we build others up? By celebrating their victories and their accomplishments. As the old saying goes, "When someone does something good, applaud—you'll make two people happy."

Genuine encouragement should never be confused with pity. God intends for His children to lead lives of abundance, joy, celebration, and praise—not lives of self-pity or regret. So we must guard ourselves against hosting (or joining) the "pity parties" that so often accompany difficult times. Instead, we must encourage each other to have faith—first in God and His only begotten Son—and then in our own abilities to use the talents God has given us for the furtherance of His kingdom and for the betterment of our own lives.

As a faithful follower of Jesus, you have every reason to be hopeful, and you have every reason to share your hopes with others. When you do, you will discover that hope, like other human emotions, is contagious. So do the world (and yourself) a favor: Look for the good in others and celebrate the good that you find. When you do, you'll be a powerful force of encouragement to your friends and family . . . and a worthy servant to your God.

The glory of friendship is not the outstretched hand,
or the kindly smile, or the joy of companionship.
It is the spiritual inspiration that comes to one when he discovers
that someone else believes in him and is willing to trust him
with his friendship.

Corrie ten Boom

Values for Life

Be a booster not a cynic: Cynicism is contagious, and so is optimism. Think and act accordingly.

Timeless Wisdom for Godly Living

So often we think that to be encouragers we have to produce great words of wisdom when, in fact, a few simple syllables of sympathy and an arm around the shoulder can often provide much needed comfort.

Florence Littauer

Those who keep speaking about the sun while walking under a cloudy sky are messengers of hope, the true saints of our day.

Henri J. Nouwen

Let's see how inventive we can be in encouraging love and helping out, not avoiding worshipping together as some do but spurring each other on.

Hebrews 10:24-25 MSG

True friends will always lift you higher and challenge you to walk in a manner pleasing to our Lord.

Lisa Bevere

A hug is the ideal gift . . . one size fits all.

Anonymous

He climbs highest who helps another up.

Zig Ziglar

More Words from God's Word

Watch the way you talk. Let nothing foul or dirty come out of your mouth. Say only what helps, each word a gift.

Ephesians 4:29 MSG

Let the word of Christ dwell in you richly in all wisdom; teaching and admonishing one another in psalms and hymns and spiritual songs, singing with grace in your hearts to the Lord.

Colossians 3:16 KJV

Encourage each other. Live in harmony and peace. Then the God of love and peace will be with you.

2 Corinthians 13:11 NLT

So encourage each other and give each other strength, just as you are doing now.

1 Thessalonians 5:11 NCV

My Values for Life

	Check Your Value		
	High	Med.	Low
I believe that God wants me to encourage other people . . .	___	___	___
I carefully think about the words I speak so that every word might be a "gift of encouragement" to others.	___	___	___
My words reflect my heart. I will guard my heart so that my words will be pleasing to God . . .	___	___	___

Whoever Loves the Father

Whoever believes that Jesus is the Christ is born of God, and whoever loves the Father loves the child born of Him.

1 John 5:1 NASB

Do you value your relationship with God . . . and do you tell Him many times each day? Hopefully so. But if you find yourself overwhelmed by the demands of everyday life, you may find yourself scurrying from place to place with scarcely a spare moment to think about your relationship with the Creator. If so, you're simply too busy for your own good.

God calls each of us to worship Him, to obey His commandments, and to accept His Son as our Savior. When we do, God blesses us in ways that we can scarcely understand. But, when we allow the demands of the day to interfere with our communications with the Father, we unintentionally distance ourselves from our greatest source of abundance and peace.

C. S. Lewis observed, "A man's spiritual health is exactly proportional to his love for God." If we are to enjoy the spiritual health that God intends for us, we must praise Him, we must love Him, and we must obey Him.

When we worship God faithfully and obediently, we invite His love into our hearts. When we truly worship God, we allow Him to rule over our days and our lives. In turn, we grow to love God even more deeply as we sense His love for us.

St. Augustine wrote, "I love you, Lord, not doubtingly, but with absolute certainty. Your Word beat upon my heart until I fell in love with you, and now the universe and everything in it tells me to love you."

Today, open your heart to the Father. Make yourself His dutiful servant as you follow in the footsteps of His only begotten Son. And let your obedience to the Father be a fitting response to His never-ending love.

Obedience that is not motivated by love cannot produce the spiritual fruit that God wants from His children.

Warren Wiersbe

Values for Life

Express yourself . . . If you sincerely love God, don't be bashful to tell Him so. And while you're at it, don't be bashful to tell other people about your feelings. If you love God, say so!

Timeless Wisdom for Godly Living

If you love God enough to ask Him what *you* can do for *Him*, then your relationship is growing deep.

Stormie Omartian

Give me, good Lord, such a love for You
that I will love nothing in a way that displeases You,
and I will love everything for Your sake.

St. Thomas More

I have a divided heart, trying to love God and the world at the same time. God says, "You can't love me as you should if you love this world too."

Mary Morrison Suggs

Whoever does not love does not know God, because God is love.

1 John 4:8 NIV

The enjoyment of God is the only happiness with which our souls can be satisfied.

Jonathan Edwards

More Words from God's Word

For this is the love of God, that we keep His commandments. And His commandments are not burdensome.

1 John 5:3 NKJV

You shall love the LORD your God with all your heart and with all your soul and with all your might.

Deuteronomy 6:5 NASB

I will sing of the LORD'S great love forever; with my mouth I will make your faithfulness known through all generations.

Psalm 89:1 NIV

And we know that in all things God works for the good of those who love him, who have been called according to his purpose.

Romans 8:28 NIV

My Values for Life

	Check Your Value		
	High	Med.	Low
In response to His great love for me, I love God . . .	___	___	___
I understand that obedience is one way of expressing my love for God . . .	___	___	___
I believe that loving God is more than a feeling. I must love God with my heart, soul, *and* mind.	___	___	___

You Are the Light

You are the light of the world. A city on a hill cannot be hidden.
Neither do people light a lamp and put it under a bowl.
Instead they put it on its stand, and it gives light to everyone in the house.
In the same way, let your light shine before men,
that they may see your good deeds and praise your Father in heaven.

Matthew 5:14-16 NIV

Are you a bashful Christian, one who is afraid to speak up for your Savior? Do you allow others to share their testimonies while you stand on the sidelines, reluctant to share yours? After His resurrection, Jesus addressed His disciples:

> But the eleven disciples proceeded to Galilee, to the mountain which Jesus had designated. When they saw Him, they worshiped Him; but some were doubtful. And Jesus came up and spoke to them, saying, "All authority has been given to Me in heaven and on earth. Go therefore and make disciples of all the nations, baptizing them in the name of the Father and the Son and the Holy Spirit, teaching them to observe all that I commanded you; and lo, I am with you always, even to the end of the age." (Matthew 28:16-20 NASB)

Christ's great commission applies to Christians of every generation, including our own. As believers, we are called to share the

Good News of Jesus Christ with our families, with our neighbors, and with the world. Yet many of us are slow to obey the last commandment of the risen Christ; we simply don't do our best to "make disciples of all the nations." Although our personal testimonies are vitally important, we sometimes hesitate to share our experiences. And that's unfortunate.

Billy Graham observed, "Our faith grows by expression. If we want to keep our faith, we must share it." If you are a follower of Christ, the time to express your belief in Him is now.

You know how Jesus has touched your heart; help Him do the same for others. You must do likewise, and you must do so today. Tomorrow may indeed be too late.

God had an only Son and He made Him a missionary.

David Livingstone

Values for Life

Don't be embarrassed to discuss your faith: You need not have attended seminary to have worthwhile opinions about your faith. Express those opinions, especially to your children; your kids need to know where you stand.

Timeless Wisdom for Godly Living

Missions is God finding those whose hearts are right with Him and placing them where they can make a difference for His kingdom.

Henry Blackaby

Being an extrovert isn't essential to evangelism—obedience and love are.

Rebecca Manley Pippert

How many people have you made homesick for God?

Oswald Chambers

Now then we are ambassadors for Christ . . . .

2 Corinthians 5:20 KJV

Go. This is the command of our Lord. Where? To the world, for it is the world that is on God's heart. Out there are multitudes for whom Christ died. And the minute you and I receive the light of the gospel, we, at that moment, become responsible for spreading that light to those who are still in darkness. Granted, we cannot all go physically, but we can go on our knees.

Kay Arthur

If you are a Christian, then you are a minister. A non-ministering Christian is a contradiction in terms.

Elton Trueblood

More Words from God's Word

And when the Holy Spirit comes on you, you will be able to be my witnesses in Jerusalem, all over Judea and Samaria, even to the ends of the world.

Acts 1:8 MSG

I will also make You a light of the nations so that My salvation may reach to the end of the earth.

Isaiah 49:6 NASB

Then Jesus came to them and said, "All authority in heaven and on earth has been given to me. Therefore go and make disciples of all nations, baptizing them in the name of the Father and of the Son and of the Holy Spirit, and teaching them to obey everything I have commanded you. And surely I am with you always, to the very end of the age."

Matthew 28:18-20 NIV

My Values for Life

	Check Your Value		
	High	Med.	Low
For me, the importance of sharing the Gospel message is . . .	___	___	___
I believe that God will empower me to share my faith . . .	___	___	___
I try to be sensitive to unplanned opportunities to share the Good News of Jesus Christ . . .	___	___	___

Possibilities . . . According to God

For with God nothing will be impossible.

Luke 1:37 NKJV

Much has been written about a harsh economic reality: Too many people live below the "poverty line." But, when we turn our thoughts from economics to religion, we must conclude that we live in a world where spiritual poverty is an even greater problem than fiscal poverty. How, then, can we assess the level of our spiritual riches, or lack thereof? In part, by measuring the faith we place in God.

Too many Christians live below the "miracle line," mistakenly limiting themselves as they mistakenly limit God. We human beings have a strange disinclination to believe in things that are beyond our meager abilities to understand. We read of God's miraculous works in Biblical times, but we tell ourselves, "That was then, and this is now." When we do so, we are mistaken. God is with His children "now" just as He was "then." He is right here, right now, performing miracles. And, He will continue to work miracles in our lives to the extent we are willing to trust in Him and to the extent those miracles fit into the fabric of His divine plan.

Miracles—both great and small—happen around us all day every day, but, usually, we're too busy to notice. Some miracles, like the twinkling of a star or the glory of a sunset, we take for granted.

Other miracles, like the healing of a terminally sick patient, we chalk up to fate or to luck. We assume, quite incorrectly, that God is "out there" and we are "right here." Nothing could be farther from the truth.

Do you lack the faith that God can work miracles in your own life? If so, it's time to reconsider. Are you living below the miracle line? If so, you are attempting to place limitations on a God who has none. Instead, trust God and His power and His miracles. And then, wait patiently . . . something miraculous is about to happen.

He who trusts in himself is lost.
He who trusts in God can do all things.

Alphonsus Liguori

Values for Life

If you're looking for miracles . . . you'll find them. If you're not, you won't.

Timeless Wisdom for Godly Living

You were born with tremendous potential.
When you were born again through faith in Jesus Christ,
God added spiritual gifts to your natural talents.

Warren Wiersbe

No eye has seen, no ear has heard,
no mind has conceived what
God has prepared for those who love him.

1 Corinthians 2:9 NIV

When you believe that nothing significant can happen through you,
you have said more about your belief in God
than you have said about yourself.

Henry Blackaby

Everyone has inside himself a piece of good news!
The good news is that you really don't know how great you can be,
how much you can live, what you can accomplish,
and what your potential is.

Anne Frank

When you say a situation or a person is hopeless,
you are slamming the door in the face of God.

Charles L. Allen

More Words from God's Word

Is anything too hard for the LORD?

Genesis 18:14 NKJV

If you have faith as a mustard seed, you will say to this mountain, "Move from here to there," and it will move; and nothing will be impossible for you.

Matthew 17:20 NKJV

I am able to do all things through Him who strengthens me.

Philippians 4:13 HCSB

If God be for us, who can be against us?

Romans 8:31 KJV

The things which are impossible with men are possible with God.

Luke 18:27 KJV

My Values for Life

	Check Your Value		
	High	Med.	Low
I expect God to work miracles . . .	___	___	___
When I place my faith in God, life becomes a grand adventure . . .	___	___	___
Worship reminds me of the awesome power of God. I worship Him daily, and seek to allow Him to work through me . . .	___	___	___

Above and Beyond Anger

Foolish people lose their tempers, but wise people control theirs.

Proverbs 29:11 NCV

Because we are imperfect human beings living among other imperfect human beings, we encounter countless frustrations, some great and some small. On occasion, we confront imminent evil, and when we do, we should respond vigorously and without reservation. But more often than not, our challenges are much more mundane. We are confronted not by impending evil but by the inevitable distractions and disappointments of life here on earth: jammed traffic, spilled coffee, and similar inconveniences. Our challenge is this: to display anger when it is appropriate and to rein in our tempers when it is not.

How can we learn to maintain better control over our tempers? By using focus, forgiveness, and faith. We must learn to focus our thoughts not on the inevitable disappointments of life but instead upon the innumerable blessings that God has given us (Philippians 4:8). In other words, we must learn to look carefully at the donut not the hole. And we must learn to forgive. When we forgive others thoroughly and often, we avoid the anger-provoking traps of bitterness and regret. Faith, too, is an antidote to anger. When we allow our faith in God to become the cornerstone and the touchstone of our lives, we cultivate an unwavering trust in the righteousness of His plans. When we do so, we begin to see God's hand as it works in every aspect of our lives—in good times and in hard times—as He uses every circumstance to fulfill His plan for us.

Sometimes we are victims of secondhand anger. We may become angry because someone else is angry. Why does this occur? Because anger is a highly contagious emotion. When we spend time with angry people, we, too, tend to become angry. Once again, God's Word offers a solution that doubles as a warning: "Make no friendship with an angry man" (Proverbs 22:24 NKJV).

The next time you are tempted to lose your temper over the minor inconveniences of life, don't. Turn away from angry people and angry thoughts. Turn instead to God. Choose forgiveness instead of hatred; choose acceptance not regret; let the assurance of God's eternal promises overcome the inevitability of life's fleeting disappointments. When you do, you'll give yourself a priceless gift: the gift of peace. And God will smile.

Anger is the noise of the soul; the unseen irritant of the heart; the relentless invader of silence.

Max Lucado

Values for Life

Time Out! If you become angry, the time to step away from the situation is before you say unkind words or do unkind things—not after. It's perfectly okay to place yourself in "time out" until you can calm down.

Timeless Wisdom for Godly Living

Acrid bitterness inevitably seeps into the lives of people who harbor grudges and suppress anger, and bitterness is always a poison.

Lee Strobel

Anger is a kind of temporary madness.

St. Basil the Great

When you are angry, do not sin,
and be sure to stop being angry before the end of the day.
Do not give the devil a way to defeat you.

Ephesians 4:26-27 NCV

Take no action in a furious passion. It's putting to sea in a storm.

Thomas Fuller

The only justifiable anger defends the great, glorious, and holy nature of our God.

John MacArthur

Why lose your temper if, by doing so, you offend God, annoy other people, give yourself a bad time . . . and, in the end, have to find it again?

Josemaria Escriva

More Words from God's Word

Now you must rid yourselves of all such things as these: anger, rage, malice . . . .

Colossians 3:8 NIV

Therefore I want the men in every place to pray, lifting up holy hands, without wrath and dissension.

1 Timothy 2:8 NASB

My dear brothers and sisters, always be willing to listen and slow to speak. Do not become angry easily, because anger will not help you live the right kind of life God wants.

James 1:19-20 NCV

Then Jesus went into the temple of God and drove out all those who bought and sold in the temple, and overturned the tables of the money changers and the seats of those who sold doves.

Matthew 21:12 NKJV

My Values for Life

	Check Your Value		
	High	Med.	Low
The importance that I place on controlling my temper . . .	___	___	___
The importance of accepting my past and forgiving those who have hurt me . . .	___	___	___
When I forgive others, I feel better about myself . . .	___	___	___

Making Choices That Please God

Our only goal is to please God whether we live here or there, because we must all stand before Christ to be judged.

2 Corinthians 5:9-10 NCV

Life is a series of choices. From the instant we wake in the morning until the moment we nod off to sleep at night, we make countless decisions: decisions about the things we do, decisions about the words we speak, and decisions about the thoughts we choose to think. Simply put, the quality of those decisions determines the quality of our lives.

As believers who have been saved by a loving and merciful God, we have every reason to make wise choices. Yet sometimes, amid the inevitable hustle and bustle of life here on earth, we allow ourselves to behave in ways that we know are displeasing to our Creator. When we do, we forfeit the joy and the peace that we might otherwise experience through Him.

As you consider the next step in your life's journey, take time to consider how many things in this life you can control: your thoughts, your words, your priorities, and your actions, for starters. And then, if you sincerely want to discover God's purpose for your life, make choices that are pleasing to Him. He deserves no less . . . and neither do you.

Sometimes, because you're an imperfect human being, you may become so wrapped up in meeting society's expectations that you fail to focus on God's expectations. To do so is a mistake of major proportions—don't make it. Instead, seek God's guidance as you focus your energies on becoming the best "you" that you can possibly be. And, when it comes to matters of conscience, seek approval not from your peers but from your Creator.

Whom will you try to please today: God or man? Your primary obligation is not to please imperfect men and women. Your obligation is to strive diligently to meet the expectations of an all-knowing and perfect God. Trust Him always. Love Him always. Praise Him always. And make choices that please Him. Always.

If you really want to please God and intend to be in full agreement with His will, you can't go wrong.

Francis Mary Paul Libermann

Values for Life

Whose plans? God's plans! If you have been struggling against God's will for your life, you have invited unwelcome consequences into your own life and into the lives of your loved ones. A far better strategy is to consult God earnestly and often. God's plans are the best plans for you.

Timeless Wisdom for Godly Living

We shouldn't work towards being saints, but to please God.

St. Thérèse of Lisieux

Make God's will the focus of your life day by day.
If you seek to please Him and Him alone,
you'll find yourself satisfied with life.

Kay Arthur

*Obviously, I'm not trying to be a people pleaser!
No, I am trying to please God. If I were still trying
to please people, I would not be Christ's servant.*

Galatians 1:10 NLT

All our offerings, whether music or martyrdom, are like
the intrinsically worthless present of a child,
which a father values indeed, but values only for the intention.

C. S. Lewis

If you are receiving your affirmation, love, self-worth, joy, strength and
acceptance from anywhere but God, He will shake it.

Lisa Bevere

You should forget about trying to be popular with everybody and
start trying to be popular with God Almighty.

Sam Jones

More Words from God's Word

. . . not my will, but thine, be done.

Luke 22:42 KJV

It is God who is at work in you,
both to will and to work for His good pleasure.

Philippians 2:13 NASB

Teach me Your way, O LORD; I will walk in Your truth.

Psalm 86:11 NKJV

Choose for yourselves today the one you will worship . . . .
As for me and my family, we will worship the LORD.

Joshua 24:15 HCSB

My Values for Life

	Check Your Value		
	High	Med.	Low
The importance of making choices that are pleasing to God . . .	___	___	___
I trust that I can please God by being obedient to His Word . . .	___	___	___
By making wise choices, I demonstrate my love for God . . .	___	___	___

Valuing Your Gifts

Each one has his own gift from God,
one in this manner and another in that.

1 Corinthians 7:7 NKJV

All of us have special talents, and you are no exception. But your talent is no guarantee of success; it must be cultivated and nurtured; otherwise, it will go unused . . . and God's gift to you will be squandered.

God knew precisely what He was doing when He gave you a unique set of talents and opportunities. And now, God wants you to use those talents for the glory of His kingdom. But you live in a world that often encourages you to do otherwise.

You inhabit a world that is filled to the brim with countless opportunities to squander your time, your resources, and your talents. So you must be watchful for distractions and temptations that might lead you astray.

Your particular talent is a treasure on temporary loan from God. He intends that your talent enrich the world and enrich your life. If you're sincerely interested in building a better life, build it upon the talents that God (in His infinite wisdom) has given you. Don't try to build a career (or a life) around the talents *you wish* He had given you.

God has blessed you with unique opportunities to serve Him, and He has given you every tool that you need to do so. Today, accept this challenge: value the talent that God has given you, nourish it, make it grow, and share it with the world. After all, the best way to say "Thank You" for God's gifts is to use them.

In the great orchestra we call life, you have an instrument and a song, and you owe it to God to play them both sublimely.

Max Lucado

Values for Life

Polishing your skills requires effort: Converting raw talent into polished skill usually requires work and lots of it. God's Word clearly instructs you to do the hard work of refining your talents for the glory of His kingdom and the service of His people. So, we are wise to remember the old adage: "What you are is God's gift to you; what you become is your gift to God." And it's up to you to make sure that *your* gift is worthy of the Giver.

Timeless Wisdom for Godly Living

Discipline is the refining fire by which talent becomes ability.

Roy L. Smith

You are the only person on earth who can use your ability.

Zig Ziglar

One thing taught large in the Holy Scriptures is that while God gives His gifts freely, He will require a strict accounting of them at the end of the road. Each man is personally responsible for his store, be it large or small, and will be required to explain his use of it before the judgment seat of Christ.

A. W. Tozer

God often reveals His direction for our lives through the way He made us . . . with a certain personality and unique skills.

Bill Hybels

Employ whatever God has entrusted you with, in doing good, all possible good, in every possible kind and degree.

John Wesley

God has given gifts to each of you from his great variety of spiritual gifts. Manage them well so that God's generosity can flow through you.

1 Peter 4:10 NLT

More Words from God's Word

Every good gift and every perfect gift is from above, and cometh down from the Father of lights.

James 1:17 KJV

The man who had received the five talents brought the other five. "Master," he said, "you entrusted me with five talents. See, I have gained five more." His master replied, "Well done, good and faithful servant! You have been faithful with a few things; I will put you in charge of many things. Come and share your master's happiness."

Matthew 25:20-21 NIV

We have different gifts, according to the grace given us. If a man's gift is prophesying, let him use it in proportion to his faith. If it is serving, let him serve; if it is teaching, let him teach; if it is encouraging, let him encourage; if it is contributing to the needs of others, let him give generously; if it is leadership, let him govern diligently; if it is showing mercy, let him do it cheerfully.

Romans 12:6-8 NIV

My Values for Life

	Check Your Value		
	High	Med.	Low
The value that I place on the gifts that God has given me . . .	___	___	___
I look for ways to cultivate my gifts and my talents . . .	___	___	___
I believe that my skills should be used in God's work . . .	___	___	___

The Beliefs That Shape Your Values

Walk in a manner worthy of the God who calls you into His own kingdom and glory.

1 Thessalonians 2:12 NASB

In describing our beliefs, our actions are far better descriptors than our words. Yet far too many of us spend more energy *talking* about our beliefs than *living* by them—with predictably poor results.

As believers, we must beware: Our actions should always give credence to the changes that Christ can make in the lives of those who walk with Him.

Your beliefs shape your values, and your values shape your life. Is your life a clearly-crafted picture book of your creed? Are your actions always consistent with your beliefs? Are you willing to practice the philosophies that you preach? Hopefully so; otherwise, you'll be tormented by inconsistencies between your beliefs and your behaviors.

If you'd like to partake in the peace that only God can give, make certain that your actions are guided by His Word. And while you're at it, pay careful attention to the conscience that God, in His infinite wisdom, has placed in your heart. Don't treat your faith as if it were separate from your everyday life. Weave your beliefs into the very fabric of your day. When you do, God will honor your good works, and your good works will honor God.

If you seek to be a responsible believer, you must realize that it is never enough to hear the instructions of God; you must also live by them. And it is never enough to wait idly by while others do God's work here on earth; you, too, must act. Doing God's work is a responsibility that every Christian (including you) should bear. And when you do, your loving Heavenly Father will reward your efforts with a bountiful harvest.

God's presence is with you, but you have to make a choice to believe—and I mean, really believe—that this is true. This conscious decision is yours alone.

Bill Hybels

Values for Life

Talking about your beliefs is easy. But, making your actions match your words is much harder. Nevertheless, if you really want to be honest with yourself, then you must make your actions match your beliefs. Period.

Timeless Wisdom for Godly Living

I believe in Christianity as I believe that the sun has risen, not only because I see it but because by it I see everything else.

C. S. Lewis

These things I have written to you who believe in the name of the Son of God, that you may know that you have eternal life.

1 John 5:13 NKJV

One man with beliefs is equal to a thousand with only interests.

John Stuart Mill

First thing every morning before you arise, say out loud, "I believe," three times.

Norman Vincent Peale

Immediately the father of the child cried out and said with tears, "Lord, I believe; help my unbelief!"

Mark 9:24 NKJV

This whole matter of Christian living is simply one issue: believing God.

Vance Havner

More Words from God's Word

I tell you the truth, whoever believes in me will do the same things that I do.
Those who believe will do even greater things than these,
because I am going to the Father.

John 14:12 NCV

Jesus turned and saw the woman and said,
"Be encouraged, dear woman. You are made well because you believed."
And the woman was healed from that moment on.

Matthew 9:22 NCV

Your beliefs about these things should be kept secret between you and God.
People are happy if they can do what they think is right
without feeling guilty.

Romans 14:22 NCV

My Values for Life

	Check Your Value		
	High	Med.	Low
The importance of making my actions consistent with my beliefs . . .	___	___	___
When I struggle with my faith or with my behavior, I take those struggles to God . . .	___	___	___
I do not believe because I see and understand; I see and understand because I believe . . .	___	___	___

Pointing Your Thoughts in the Right Direction

Finally brothers, whatever is true, whatever is honorable, whatever is just, whatever is pure, whatever is lovely, whatever is commendable— if there is any moral excellence and if there is any praise— dwell on these things.

Philippians 4:8 HCSB

How will you direct your thoughts today? Will you be an upbeat believer? Will you be a person whose hopes and dreams are alive and well? Will you put a smile on your face and a song in your heart? Hopefully so. But here's a word of warning: sometimes, when pessimism, anger, or doubt threaten to hijack your emotions, you won't feel much like celebrating. That's why you must always strive to keep your thoughts headed in the right direction.

Your thoughts have the power to lift you up or drag you down; they have the power to energize you or deplete you, to inspire you to greater accomplishments or to make those accomplishments impossible.

What kind of attitude will you select today? Will you obey the words of Philippians 4:7-8 by dwelling upon those things that are "true and honorable and right"? Or will you allow yourself to be swayed by the negativity that seems to dominate our troubled world?

God intends that you experience joy and abundance, but He will not force His joy upon you; you must claim it for yourself. It's up to you to celebrate the life that God has given you by focusing your mind upon "things that are excellent and worthy of praise." So today, spend more time thinking about your blessings and less time fretting about your hardships. Then, take time to thank the Giver of all things good for gifts that are, in truth, far too numerous to count.

We know well enough how to keep outward silence, and to hush our spoken words, but we know little of interior silence. It consists in hushing our idle, restless, wandering imagination, in quieting the promptings of our worldly minds, and in suppressing the crowd of unprofitable thoughts which excite and disturb the soul.

François Fènelon

Values for Life

Watch what you think: If your inner voice is, in reality, your inner critic, you need to tone down the criticism now. And while you're at it, train yourself to begin thinking thoughts that are more rational, more accepting, and less judgmental. (Philippians 4:8)

Timeless Wisdom for Godly Living

The things we think are the things that feed our souls. If we think on pure and lovely things, we shall grow pure and lovely like them; and the converse is equally true.

Hannah Whitall Smith

So prepare your minds for service and have self-control.

1 Peter 1:13 NCV

Our own possible bad thoughts and deeds are far more dangerous to us than any enemy from the world.

St. Ambrose

If our minds are stayed upon God, His peace will rule the affairs entertained by our minds. If, on the other hand, we allow our minds to dwell on the cares of this world, God's peace will be far from our thoughts.

Woodroll Kroll

No more imperfect thoughts. No more sad memories. No more ignorance. My redeemed body will have a redeemed mind. Grant me a foretaste of that perfect mind as you mirror your thoughts in me today.

Joni Eareckson Tada

More Words from God's Word

Set your mind on the things above, not on the things that are on earth.

Colossians 3:2 NASB

Come near to God, and God will come near to you. You sinners, clean sin out of your lives. You who are trying to follow God and the world at the same time, make your thinking pure.

James 4:8 NCV

Those who are pure in their thinking are happy, because they will be with God.

Matthew 5:8 NCV

May the words of my mouth and the thoughts of my heart be pleasing to you, O LORD, my rock and my redeemer.

Psalm 19:14 NLT

My Values for Life

	Check Your Value		
	High	Med.	Low
The importance that I place on the need to direct my thoughts in the proper direction . . .	___	___	___
I believe that emotions are contagious, so I try to associate with people who are upbeat, optimistic, and encouraging . . .	___	___	___
When I dwell on positive thoughts, I feel better about myself *and* my circumstances . . .	___	___	___

The Value of Courage

The LORD is my light and my salvation; whom shall I fear? The LORD is the strength of my life; of whom shall I be afraid?

Psalm 27:1 KJV

A storm rose quickly on the Sea of Galilee, and the disciples were afraid. Although they had seen Jesus perform many miracles, although they had walked side by side with the Son of God, the disciples feared for their lives. So they turned to their Savior, and He calmed the waters and the wind.

Sometimes, we, like the disciples, feel threatened by the inevitable storms of life. When we are fearful, we, too, can turn to Christ for courage and for comfort. When we do so, He calms our fears just as surely as He calmed the winds and the waters two thousand years ago.

D. L. Moody said, "Take courage. We walk in the wilderness today and in the Promised Land tomorrow." And he is right. As believers we should walk through life's difficult days with God's promises at the forefront of our thoughts. But even the most faithful among us may feel overwhelmed at times, especially when we are tested by the inevitable disappointments and tragedies that occur in the lives of believers and non-believers alike. When we feel threatened, we must turn our thoughts and prayers to God and to His only begotten Son.

The next time you're afraid, remember that the One who calmed the wind and the waves is also your personal Savior. The next time you find your courage tested to the limit, remember that God is as near as your next breath, and remember that He offers salvation to His children. He is your shield and your strength; He is your protector and your deliverer. Call upon Him in your hour of need and then be comforted. Whatever your challenge, whatever your trouble, God can handle it. And will.

What is courage? It is the ability to be strong in trust, in conviction, in obedience. To be courageous is to step out in faith—
to trust and obey, no matter what.

Kay Arthur

Values for Life

Is your courage being tested? Cling tightly to God's promises, and pray. God can give you the strength to meet any challenge, and that's exactly what you should ask Him to do.

Timeless Wisdom for Godly Living

A man who is intimate with God will never be intimidated by men.

Leonard Ravenhill

Courage faces fear and thereby masters it.
Cowardice represses fear and is thereby mastered by it.

Martin Luther King, Jr.

Be strong and brave, and do the work.
Don't be afraid or discouraged, because the LORD God,
my God, is with you. He will not fail you or leave you.

1 Chronicles 28:20 NCV

God knows that the strength that comes from wrestling
with our fear will give us wings to fly.

Paula Rinehart

Why rely on yourself and fall? Cast yourself upon His arm.
Be not afraid. He will not let you slip. Cast yourself in confidence.
He will receive you and heal you.

St. Augustine

Are you fearful? First, bow your head and pray for God's strength.
Then, raise your head knowing that, together,
you and God can handle whatever comes your way.

Jim Gallery

More Words from God's Word

Be on guard. Stand true to what you believe. Be courageous. Be strong.

1 Corinthians 16:13 NLT

For God has not given us a spirit of fearfulness, but one of power, love, and sound judgment.

2 Timothy 1:7 HCSB

The LORD himself goes before you and will be with you; he will never leave you nor forsake you. Do not be afraid; do not be discouraged.

Deuteronomy 31:8 NIV

Do not be afraid . . . I am your shield, your very great reward.

Genesis 15:1 NIV

I can do everything through him that gives me strength.

Philippians 4:13 NIV

My Values for Life

For me, the value of living courageously is . . .

I overcome fear by praying, and then by facing my fears head on . . .

When I find myself in a situation that I cannot control, I turn my concerns over to God and leave the results up to Him . . .

Check Your Value		
High	Med.	Low
___	___	___
___	___	___
___	___	___

Courage

Finding Contentment in a Discontented World

But godliness with contentment is great gain.
For we brought nothing into the world, and we can take nothing out of it.
But if we have food and clothing, we will be content with that.

1 Timothy 6:6-8 NIV

When we conduct ourselves in ways that are opposed to God's commandments, we rob ourselves of God's peace. When we fall prey to the temptations and distractions of our irreverent age, we rob ourselves of God's blessings. When we become preoccupied with material possessions or personal status, we forfeit the contentment that is rightfully ours in Christ.

Where can we find lasting contentment? Is it a result of wealth or power or fame? Hardly. Genuine contentment is a gift from God to those who follow His commandments and accept His Son. When Christ dwells at the center of our families and our lives, contentment will belong to us just as surely as we belong to Him.

Do you seek happiness, abundance, and contentment? If so, here are some things you should do: Love God and His Son; depend upon God for strength; try, to the best of your abilities, to follow God's will; and strive to obey His Holy Word. When you do these things, you'll discover that happiness goes hand-in-hand with righteousness. The happiest people are not those who rebel against God; the happiest people are those who love God and obey His commandments.

What does life have in store for you? A world full of possibilities (of course it's up to you to seize them) and God's promise of abundance (of course it's up to you to accept it). So, as you embark upon the next phase of your journey, remember to celebrate the life that God has given you. Your Creator has blessed you beyond measure. Honor Him with your prayers, your words, your deeds, and your joy.

Are you a thoroughly contented Christian? If so, then you are well aware of the healing power of the risen Christ. But if your spirit is temporarily troubled, perhaps you need to focus less upon your own priorities and more upon God's priorities. When you do, you'll rediscover this life-changing truth: Genuine contentment begins with God . . . and ends there.

True contentment comes from godliness in the heart,
not from wealth in the hand.

Warren Wiersbe

Values for Life

Be contented where you are . . . even if it's not exactly where you want to end up. God has something wonderful in store for you—and remember that God's timing is perfect—so be patient, trust God, do your best, and expect the best.

Timeless Wisdom for Godly Living

We will never be happy until we make God the source
of our fulfillment and the answer to our longings.

Stormie Omartian

If the grass is greener on the other side, fertilize yours.

Anonymous

The heart is rich when it is content, and it is content
when its desires are set upon God.

Miguel of Ecuador

*Satisfy us in the morning with your unfailing love,
that we may sing for joy and be glad all our days.*

Psalm 90:14 NIV

The most powerful life is the most simple life.
The most powerful life is the life that knows where it's going,
that knows where the source of strength is; it is the life that stays
free of clutter and happenstance and hurriedness.

Max Lucado

The secret of contentment in the midst of change is found
in having roots in the changeless Christ—
the same yesterday, today and forever.

Ed Young

More Words from God's Word

I know what it is to be in need, and I know what it is to have plenty. I have learned the secret of being content in any and every situation, whether well fed or hungry, whether living in plenty or in want. I can do everything through him who gives me strength.

Philippians 4:12-13 NIV

Keep your lives free from the love of money and be content with what you have, because God has said, "Never will I leave you; never will I forsake you."

Hebrews 13:5 NIV

If they obey and serve him, they will spend the rest of their days in prosperity and their years in contentment.

Job 36:11 NIV

I have learned to be content whatever the circumstances.

Philippians 4:11 NIV

My Values for Life

	Check Your Value		
	High	Med.	Low
For me, the importance that I place on being contented is . . .	___	___	___
I understand that contentment comes not from my circumstances but from my attitude . . .	___	___	___
I believe that peace with God is the starting point for a contented life . . .	___	___	___

The Value of Hope

Be of good courage, and He shall strengthen your heart,
all you who hope in the LORD.

Psalm 31:24 NKJV

On the darkest days of our lives, we may be confronted with an illusion that seems very real indeed: the illusion of hopelessness. Try though we might, we simply can't envision a solution to our problems—and we fall into the darkness of despair. During these times, we may question God—His love, His presence, even His very existence. Despite God's promises, despite Christ's love, and despite our many blessings, we may envision little or no hope for the future. These dark days can be dangerous times for us and for our loved ones.

If you find yourself falling into the spiritual traps of worry and discouragement, seek the encouraging words of fellow Christians, and the healing touch of Jesus. After all, it was Christ who promised, "These things I have spoken unto you, that in me ye might have peace. In the world ye shall have tribulation: but be of good cheer; I have overcome the world" (John 16:33 KJV).

Can you place your future into the hands of a loving and all-knowing God? Can you live amid the uncertainties of today, knowing that God has dominion over all your tomorrows? Can you summon the faith to trust God in good times and hard times? If you can, you are wise and you are blessed.

Once you've made the decision to trust God completely,

it's time to get busy. The willingness to take action—even if the outcome of that action is uncertain—is an effective way to combat hopelessness. When you decide to roll up your sleeves and begin solving your own problems, you'll feel empowered, and you may see the first real glimmer of hope.

If you're waiting for someone else to solve your problems, or if you're waiting for God to patch things up by Himself, you may become impatient, despondent, or both. But when you stop waiting and start working, God has a way of pitching in and finishing the job. The advice of American publisher Cyrus Curtis still rings true: "Believe in the Lord and he will do half the work—the last half."

So, today and every day, ask God for these things: clear perspective, mountain-moving faith, and the courage to do what needs doing. After all, no problem is too big for God—not even yours.

Easter comes each year to remind us of a truth that is eternal and universal. The empty tomb of Easter morning says to you and me, "Of course you'll encounter trouble. But behold a God of power who can take any evil and turn it into a door of hope."

Catherine Marshall

Values for Life

Remember: other people have experienced the same kind of hard times you may be experiencing now. They made it, and so can you. (Psalm 146:5)

Timeless Wisdom for Godly Living

When you say a situation or a person is hopeless,
you are slamming the door in the face of God.

Charles L. Allen

Hope is the desire and the ability to move forward.

Emilie Barnes

The hope we have in Jesus is the anchor for the soul—something sure and steadfast, preventing drifting or giving way, lowered to the depth of God's love.

Franklin Graham

Oh, remember this: There is never a time when we may not hope in God. Whatever our necessities, however great our difficulties, and though to all appearance help is impossible, yet our business is to hope in God, and it will be found that it is not in vain.

George Mueller

Those who keep speaking about the sun while walking under a cloudy sky are messengers of hope, the true saints of our day.

Henri J. Nouwen

Therefore we do not lose heart.
Even though our outward man is perishing,
yet the inward man is being renewed day by day.

2 Corinthians 4:16 NKJV

More Words from God's Word

Without wavering, let us hold tightly to the hope we say we have, for God can be trusted to keep his promise.

Hebrews 10:23 NLT

Now faith is the substance of things hoped for, the evidence of things not seen.

Hebrews 11:1 KJV

This hope we have as an anchor of the soul, a hope both sure and steadfast.

Hebrews 6:19 NASB

Relax, everything's going to be all right; rest, everything's coming together; open your hearts, love is on the way!

Jude 1:2 MSG

Happy is he . . . whose hope is in the L*ORD* *his God.*

Psalm 146:5 KJV

My Values for Life

	Check Your Value		
	High	Med.	Low
I believe that genuine hope begins with hope in a sovereign God . . .	___	___	___
I have found that action is an antidote to worry . . .	___	___	___
I believe that God offers me "a peace that passes understanding," and I desire to accept God's peace . . .	___	___	___

The Power of Patience

Knowing God leads to self-control. Self-control leads to patient endurance, and patient endurance leads to godliness.

2 Peter 1:6 NLT

The dictionary defines the word *patience* as "the ability to be calm, tolerant, and understanding." If that describes you, you can skip the rest of this page. But, if you're like most of us, you'd better keep reading.

For most of us, patience is a hard thing to master. Why? Because we have lots of things we want, and we know precisely when we want them: NOW (if not sooner). But our Father in heaven has other ideas; the Bible teaches that we must learn to wait patiently for the things that God has in store for us, even when waiting is difficult.

We live in an imperfect world inhabited by imperfect people. Sometimes, we inherit troubles from others, and sometimes we create troubles for ourselves. On other occasions, we see other people "moving ahead" in the world, and we want to move ahead with them. So we become impatient with ourselves, with our circumstances, and even with our Creator.

Psalm 37:7 commands us to "rest in the LORD, and wait patiently for Him" (NKJV). But, for most of us, waiting patiently for Him is hard. We are fallible human beings who seek solutions to our problems today, not tomorrow. Still, God instructs us to wait patiently for His plans to unfold, and that's exactly what we should do.

Sometimes, patience is the price we pay for being responsible adults, and that's as it should be. After all, think how patient our Heavenly Father has been with us. So the next time you find yourself drumming your fingers as you wait for a quick resolution to the challenges of everyday living, take a deep breath and ask God for patience. Be still before your Heavenly Father and trust His timetable: it's the peaceful way to live.

Waiting means going about our assigned tasks,
confident that God will provide the meaning and the conclusions.

Eugene Peterson

Values for Life

The best things in life seldom happen overnight . . . Henry Blackaby writes, "The grass that is here today and gone tomorrow does not require much time to mature. A big oak tree that lasts for generations requires much more time to grow and mature. God is concerned about your life through eternity. Allow Him to take all the time He needs to shape you for His purposes. Larger assignments will require longer periods of preparation." How true!

Timeless Wisdom for Godly Living

No matter what we are going through, no matter how long the waiting for answers, of one thing we may be sure. God is faithful. He keeps His promises. What He starts, He finishes . . . including His perfect work in us.

Gloria Gaither

But if we look forward to something we don't have yet, we must wait patiently and confidently.

Romans 8:25 NLT

Be patient. When you feel lonely, stay with your loneliness. Avoid the temptation to let your fearful self run off. Let it teach you its wisdom; let it tell you that you can live instead of just surviving. Gradually you will become one, and you will find that Jesus is living in your heart and offering you all you need.

Henri Nouwen

In the name of Jesus Christ, who was never in a hurry, we pray, O God, that You will slow us down, for we know that we live too fast. With all eternity before us, make us take time to live—time to get acquainted with You, time to enjoy Your blessing, and time to know each other.

Peter Marshall

More Words from God's Word

Patience and encouragement come from God.
And I pray that God will help you all agree with each other
the way Christ Jesus wants.

Romans 15:5 NCV

I wait quietly before God, for my salvation comes from him.
He alone is my rock and my salvation,
my fortress where I will never be shaken.

Psalm 62:1-2 NLT

For when the way is rough, your patience has a chance to grow.
So let it grow, and don't try to squirm out of your problems.

James 1:3-4 TLB

My Values for Life

	Check Your Value		
	High	Med.	Low
I take seriously the Bible's instructions to be patient . . .	___	___	___
I believe that patience is not idle waiting but that it is an activity that means watching and waiting for God to lead me . . .	___	___	___
Even when I don't understand the circumstances that confront me, I strive to wait patiently while serving the Lord . . .	___	___	___

The Joys of Friendship

As iron sharpens iron, a friend sharpens a friend.

Proverbs 27:17 NLT

The dictionary defines the word *friend* as "a person who is attached to another by feelings of affection or personal regard." This definition is accurate, as far as it goes, but when we examine the deeper meaning of friendship, many more descriptors come to mind: trustworthiness, loyalty, helpfulness, kindness, understanding, forgiveness, encouragement, humor, and cheerfulness, to mention but a few. Needless to say, our trusted friends and family members can help us discover God's unfolding purposes for our lives. Our task is to enlist our friends' wisdom, their cooperation, their honesty, and their encouragement.

An old familiar hymn begins, "What a friend we have in Jesus . . . ." No truer words were ever penned. Jesus is the sovereign friend and ultimate Savior of mankind. Just as Christ has been—and will always be—the ultimate friend to His flock, so should we be Christ-like in our love and devotion to our own little flock of friends and neighbors. When we share the love of Christ, we share a priceless gift. As loyal friends, we must do no less.

As you consider the many blessings that God has given you, remember to thank Him for the friends He has chosen to place along your path. Seek their guidance, and, when asked, never withhold yours. Then, as you travel through life with trusted companions by your side, you will bless them, and they will richly bless you.

Loyal Christian friendship is ordained by God. Throughout the Bible, we are reminded to love one another, to care for one another, and to treat one another as we wish to be treated. So remember the important role that Christian friendship plays in God's plans for His kingdom *and* for your life. Resolve to be a trustworthy, loyal friend. And, treasure the people in your life who are loyal friends to you. Friendship is, after all, a glorious gift, praised by God. Give thanks for that gift and nurture it.

Friendship between the friends of Jesus of Nazareth
is unlike any other friendship.

Stephen Neill

Values for Life

Remember the first rule of friendship: it's the Golden one, and it starts like this: "Do unto others . . ." (Matthew 7:12).

Timeless Wisdom for Godly Living

*Greater love has no one than this,
that he lay down his life for his friends.*
John 15:13 NIV

The bond of human friendship has a sweetness of its own, binding many souls together as one.

St. Augustine

Friendship fills a deep well within me with fresh water. When I celebrate my friendships, it's like dropping a huge rock into the well. It splashes that water everywhere, on everyone else in my life.

Nicole Johnson

Perhaps the greatest treasure on earth and one of the only things that will survive this life is human relationships: old friends. We are indeed rich if we have friends. Friends who have loved us through the problems and heartaches of life. Deep, true, joyful friendships. Life is too short and eternity too long to live without old friends.

Gloria Gaither

You must know that I should not love you half so well, if I did not believe you would be my friend for eternity. There is not room enough for friendship to unfold itself in such a nook of life as this.

William Cowper

More Words from God's Word

A friend loves you all the time, and a brother helps in time of trouble.

Proverbs 17:17 NCV

Beloved, if God so loved us, we also ought to love one another.

1 John 4:11 NKJV

So don't lose a minute in building on what you've been given, complementing your basic faith with good character, spiritual understanding, alert discipline, passionate patience, reverent wonder, warm friendliness, and generous love, each dimension fitting into and developing the others.

2 Peter 1:5-7 MSG

A man's counsel is sweet to his friend.

Proverbs 27:9 NASB

How good and pleasant it is when brothers live together in unity!

Psalm 133:1 NIV

My Values for Life

	Check Your Value		
	High	Med.	Low
For me, the value that I place on friendship is . . .	___	___	___
In building friendships, I emphasize the need for mutual honesty and mutual trust . . .	___	___	___
Because I want to cultivate my friendships, I make the effort to spend time with my friends . . .	___	___	___

The Source of Strength

But those who wait on the LORD shall renew their strength;
They shall mount up with wings like eagles,
they shall run and not be weary, they shall walk and not faint.

Isaiah 40:31 NKJV

Even the most inspired Christians can, from time to time, find themselves running on empty. The demands of daily life can drain us of our strength and rob us of the joy that is rightfully ours in Christ. When we find ourselves tired, discouraged, or worse, there is a source from which we can draw the power needed to recharge our spiritual batteries. That source is God.

God intends that His children lead joyous lives filled with abundance and peace. But sometimes, abundance and peace seem very far away. It is then that we must turn to God for renewal, and when we do, He will restore us *if* we allow Him to do so.

Today, like every other day, is literally brimming with possibilities. Whether we realize it or not, God is always working in us and through us; our job is to let Him do His work without undue interference. Yet we are imperfect beings who, because of our limited vision, often resist God's will. And oftentimes, because of our stubborn insistence on squeezing too many activities into a 24-hour day, we allow ourselves to become exhausted, or frustrated, or both.

Are you tired or troubled? Turn your heart toward God in prayer. Are you weak or worried? Take the time—or, more accurately, make the time—to delve deeply into God's Holy Word. Are you spiritually depleted? Call upon fellow believers to support you, and call upon Christ to renew your spirit and your life. Are you simply overwhelmed by the demands of the day? Pray for the wisdom to simplify your life. Are you exhausted? Pray for the wisdom to rest a little more and worry a little less.

When you do these things, you'll discover that the Creator of the universe stands always ready and always able to create a new sense of wonderment and joy in you.

No matter how badly we have failed, we can always get up and begin again. Our God is the God of new beginnings.

Warren Wiersbe

Values for Life

God is in the business of making all things new: Vance Havner correctly observed, "God is not running an antique shop! He is making all things new!" And that includes you.

Timeless Wisdom for Godly Living

Repentance removes old sins and wrong attitudes,
and it opens the way for the Holy Spirit to restore our spiritual health.

Shirley Dobson

God specializes in taking bruised, soiled, broken, guilty,
and miserable vessels and making them whole, forgiven,
and useful again.

Charles Swindoll

The same voice that brought Lazarus out of the tomb
raised us to newness of life.

C. H. Spurgeon

*But may the God of all grace, who called us
to His eternal glory by Christ Jesus,
after you have suffered a while, perfect, establish,
strengthen, and settle you.*

1 Peter 5:10 NKJV

But while relaxation is one thing, refreshment is another.
We need to drink frequently and at length from God's fresh springs, to
spend time in the Scripture, time in fellowship with Him,
time worshiping Him.

Ruth Bell Graham

More Words from God's Word

The LORD says, "Forget what happened before, and do not think about the past. Look at the new thing I am going to do. It is already happening. Don't you see it? I will make a road in the desert and rivers in the dry land.

Isaiah 43:18-19 NCV

Come to Me, all you who are weary and burdened, and I will give you rest. Take My yoke upon you and learn from Me, because I am gentle and humble in heart, and you will find rest for your souls. For My yoke is easy and My burden is light.

Matthew 11:28-30 HCSB

The LORD is my shepherd; I shall not want. He makes me to lie down in green pastures; He leads me beside the still waters. He restores my soul.

Psalm 23:1-3 NKJV

My Values for Life

	Check Your Value		
	High	Med.	Low
I believe that God can make all things new—including me . . .	___	___	___
I take time each day to be still and let God give me perspective and direction . . .	___	___	___
I understand the importance of rest and getting a good night's sleep . . .	___	___	___

Renewal

Accepting God's Forgiveness

Let us, then, feel very sure that we can come before God's throne where there is grace. There we can receive mercy and grace to help us when we need it.

Hebrews 4:16 NCV

All of us have sinned. Sometimes our sins result from our own stubborn rebellion against God's commandments. Sometimes, we are swept up by events that encourage us to behave in ways that we later come to regret. And sometimes, even when our intentions are honorable, we make mistakes that have long-lasting consequences. When we look back at our actions with remorse, we may experience intense feelings of guilt. But God has an answer for the guilt that we feel. That answer, of course, is His forgiveness.

When we genuinely repent from our wrongdoings, and when we sincerely confess our sins, we are forgiven by our Heavenly Father. But long after God has forgiven us, we may continue to withhold forgiveness from ourselves. Instead of accepting God's mercy and accepting our past, we may think long and hard—far too long and hard—about the things that "might have been," the things that "could have been," or the things that "should have been."

Are you troubled by feelings of guilt, even after you've received God's forgiveness? Are you still struggling with painful memories of mistakes you made long ago? Are you focused so intently on yesterday that your vision of today is clouded? If so, you still have work to do—spiritual work. You should ask your Heavenly Father not for forgiveness (He granted that gift the very first time you asked Him!), but instead for acceptance and trust: acceptance of the past and trust in God's plan for your life.

Once you have asked God for His forgiveness, you can be certain that your Heavenly Father has given it. And if He, in His infinite wisdom, will forgive your sins, how then can you withhold forgiveness from yourself? The answer, of course, is that once God has forgiven you, you should forgive yourself, too.

When you forgive yourself thoroughly and completely, you'll stop investing energy in those most useless of emotions: bitterness, regret, and self-recrimination. And you can then get busy making the world a better place, and that's as it should be. After all, since God has forgiven you, isn't it about time that you demonstrate your gratitude by serving Him.

We are products of our past, but we don't have to be prisoners of it. God specializes in giving people a fresh start.

Rick Warren

Values for Life

If you've asked for God's forgiveness, He has given it. But have you forgiven yourself? If not, the best moment to do so is this one.

Timeless Wisdom for Godly Living

What makes a Christian a Christian is not perfection but forgiveness.

Max Lucado

The LORD is full of compassion and mercy.

James 5:11 NIV

Forgiveness is contagious. First you forgive them, and pretty soon, they'll forgive you, too.

Marie T. Freeman

Looking back over my life, all I can see is mercy and grace written in large letters everywhere. May God help me have the same kind of heart toward those who wound or offend me.

Jim Cymbala

The LORD is gracious and full of compassion,
slow to anger and great in mercy.
The LORD is good to all,
and His tender mercies are over all His works.

Psalm 145:8-9 NKJV

God carries your picture in his wallet.

Tony Campolo

More Words from God's Word

But because of his great love for us, God, who is rich in mercy, made us alive with Christ even when we were dead in transgressions—it is by grace you have been saved.

Ephesians 2:4-5 NIV

But when the kindness and love of God our Savior appeared, he saved us, not because of righteous things we had done, but because of his mercy.

Titus 3:4-5 NIV

Be gentle with one another, sensitive. Forgive one another as quickly and thoroughly as God in Christ forgave you.

Ephesians 4:32 MSG

But when you are praying, first forgive anyone you are holding a grudge against, so that your Father in heaven will forgive your sins, too.

Mark 11:25 NLT

My Values for Life

	Check Your Value		
	High	Med.	Low
The value that I place upon God's forgiveness . . .	___	___	___
Because God has forgiven me, I can forgive myself	___	___	___
Because God has forgiven me, I can forgive others . . .	___	___	___

Discovering God's Peace

And the peace of God, which transcends all understanding,
will guard your hearts and your minds in Christ Jesus.

Philippians 4:7 NIV

Have you found the lasting peace that can—and should—be yours through Jesus Christ? Or are you still chasing the illusion of "peace and happiness" that the world promises but cannot deliver?

The beautiful words of John 14:27 promise that Jesus offers peace not as the world gives but as He alone gives: "Peace I leave with you. My peace I give to you. I do not give to you as the world gives. Your heart must not be troubled or fearful" (HCSB). Your challenge is to accept Christ's peace and then, as best you can, to share His peace with your neighbors. But sometimes, that's easier said than done.

If you are a person with lots of obligations and plenty of responsibilities, it is simply a fact of life: You worry. From time to time, you worry about finances, safety, health, home, family, or about countless other concerns, some great and some small. Where is the best place to take your worries? Take them to God . . . and leave them there.

The Scottish preacher George McDonald observed, "It has been well said that no man ever sank under the burden of the day. It is when tomorrow's burden is added to the burden of today that the weight is more than a man can bear. Never load yourselves so, my friends. If you find yourselves so loaded, at least remember this: it is your own doing, not God's. He begs you to leave the future to Him."

Today, as a gift to yourself, to your family, and to your friends, claim the inner peace that is your spiritual birthright: the peace of Jesus Christ. Christ is standing at the door, waiting patiently for you to invite Him to reign over your heart. His eternal peace is offered freely. Claim it today.

A great many people are trying to make peace,
but that has already been done. God has not left it for us to do;
all we have to do is to enter into it.

D. L. Moody

Values for Life

Whatever it is, God can handle it: Sometimes peace is a scarce commodity in a demanding, 21st-century world. How can we find the peace that we so desperately desire? By turning our days and our lives over to God. Elisabeth Elliot writes, "If my life is surrendered to God, all is well. Let me not grab it back, as though it were in peril in His hand but would be safer in mine!" May we give our lives, our hopes, and our prayers to the Father, and, by doing so, accept His will and His peace.

Timeless Wisdom for Godly Living

Peace is full confidence that God is who He says He is and that He will keep every promise in His Word.

Dorothy Harrison Pentecost

For Jesus peace seems to have meant not the absence of struggle but the presence of love.

Frederick Buechner

You, LORD, give true peace to those who depend on you, because they trust you.

Isaiah 26:3 NCV

When peace like a river attendeth my way,
When sorrows like sea billows roll;
Whatever my lot, Thou hast taught me to say,
"It is well, it is well with my soul."

Horatio G. Spafford

Where the Spirit of the Lord is, there is peace;
where the Spirit of the Lord is, there is love.

Stephen R. Adams

Great tranquility of heart is his who cares for neither praise nor blame.

Thomas à Kempis

More Words from God's Word

May the God of hope fill you with all joy and peace as you trust in him, so that you may overflow with hope by the power of the Holy Spirit.

Romans 15:13 NIV

And this righteousness will bring peace.
Quietness and confidence will fill the land forever.

Isaiah 32:17 NLT

Those who love Your law have great peace,
and nothing causes them to stumble.

Psalm 119:165 NASB

Let us therefore follow after the things which make for peace, and things wherewith one may edify another.

Romans 14:19 KJV

My Values for Life

	Check Your Value		
	High	Med.	Low
The value that I place on living a peaceful life . . .	___	___	___
Experience teaches me that peace is found by living in the center of God's will . . .	___	___	___
I find that the more time I spend in prayer, the more peaceful I feel . . .	___	___	___

The Way of the Righteous

For the LORD knows the way of the righteous,
but the way of the ungodly shall perish.

Psalm 1:6 NKJV

Oswald Chambers, the author of the Christian classic devotional text *My Utmost for His Highest*, advised, "Never support an experience which does not have God as its source, and faith in God as its result." These words serve as a powerful reminder that, as Christians, we are called to walk with God and obey His commandments. But, we live in a world that presents us with countless temptations to stray far from God's path. We Christians, when confronted with sin, have clear instructions: Walk—or better yet run—in the opposite direction.

When we seek righteousness in our own lives—and when we seek the companionship of those who do likewise—we reap the spiritual rewards that God intends for our lives. When we behave ourselves as godly men and women, we honor God. When we live righteously and according to God's commandments, He blesses us in ways that we cannot fully understand.

Each new day presents countless opportunities to put God in first place . . . or not. When we honor Him by living according to His commandments, we earn for ourselves the abundance and peace that He promises. But, when we concern ourselves more with pleasing others than with pleasing our Creator, we bring needless suffering upon ourselves and our families. Would you like a time-tested formula for successful living? Here is a formula that is proven and true: Seek God's approval in every aspect of your life. Does this sound too simple? Perhaps it is simple, but it is also the only way to reap the marvelous riches that God has in store for you.

So today, take every step of your journey with God as your traveling companion. Read His Word and follow His commandments. Support only those activities that further God's kingdom and your spiritual growth. Be an example of righteous living to your friends, to your neighbors, and to your children. Then, reap the blessings that God has promised to all those who live according to His will and His Word.

Righteousness not only defines God, but God defines righteousness.

Bill Hybels

Values for Life

Righteous living is not just for some special few but for everyone. Elisabeth Elliot writes: "Let us never suppose that obedience is impossible or that holiness is meant only for a select few. Our Shepherd leads us in paths of righteousness—not for our name's sake but for His."

Timeless Wisdom for Godly Living

If we don't hunger and thirst after righteousness,
we'll become anemic and feel miserable in our Christian experience.

Franklin Graham

But by His doing you are in Christ Jesus,
who became to us wisdom from God,
and righteousness and sanctification, and redemption.

1 Corinthians 1:30 NASB

Our souls were made to live in an upper atmosphere,
and we stifle and choke if we live on any lower level.
Our eyes were made to look off from these heavenly heights,
and our vision is distorted by any lower gazing.

Hannah Whitall Smith

Holiness is not God's asking us to be "good";
it is an invitation to be "His."

Lisa Bevere

Sanctify yourself and you will sanctify society.

St. Francis of Assisi

Simplicity reaches out after God; purity discovers and enjoys him.

Thomas à Kempis

More Words from God's Word

But now you must be holy in everything you do, just as God—who chose you to be his children—is holy. For he himself has said, "You must be holy because I am holy."

1 Peter 1:15-16 NLT

For the eyes of the LORD *are on the righteous, and His ears are open to their prayers; but the face of the* LORD *is against those who do evil.*

1 Peter 3:12 NKJV

Walk in a manner worthy of the God who calls you into His own kingdom and glory.

1 Thessalonians 2:12 NASB

Blessed are those who hunger and thirst for righteousness, for they will be filled.

Matthew 5:6 NIV

My Values for Life

	Check Your Value		
	High	Med.	Low
The value that I place upon living a life that is pleasing to God . . .	___	___	___
As my own example for living, I look to Jesus . . .	___	___	___
For me, the importance of setting a good example for my family and friends . . .	___	___	___

This Is the Day . . .

This is the day which the LORD has made; let us rejoice and be glad in it.
Psalm 118:24 NASB

The familiar words of Psalm 118 remind us that today, like every day, is a priceless gift from God. What do you expect from the day ahead? Are you expecting God to do wonderful things, or are you living beneath a cloud of apprehension and doubt? Do you expect God to use you in unexpected ways, or do you expect another uneventful day to pass with little fanfare? As a thoughtful believer, the answer to these questions should be obvious.

C. H. Spurgeon, the renowned 19th-century English clergyman, advised, "Rejoicing is clearly a spiritual command. To ignore it, I need to remind you, is disobedience." As Christians, we are called by our Creator to live abundantly, prayerfully, and joyfully. To do otherwise is to squander His spiritual gifts.

Christ came to this earth to give us abundant life and eternal salvation. Our task is to accept Christ's grace with joy in our hearts and praise on our lips. When we fashion our days around Jesus, we are transformed: we see the world differently, we act differently, and we feel differently about ourselves and our neighbors.

If you're a thoughtful Christian, then you're a thankful Christian. And because of your faith, you can face the inevitable challenges and disappointments of each day, armed with the joy of Christ and the promise of salvation.

So whatever this day holds for you, begin it and end it with God as your partner and Christ as your Savior. And throughout the day, give thanks to the One who created you and saved you. God's love for you is infinite—accept it joyfully and be thankful.

Commitment to His Lordship on Easter, at revivals, or even every Sunday is not enough. We must choose this day—and every day—whom we will serve. This deliberate act of the will is the inevitable choice between habitual fellowship and habitual failure.

Beth Moore

Values for Life

Today's Journey: Life is a journey, and today is an important part of that journey. Yet we may be tempted to take this day—along with the ones that precede it and the ones that follow it—for granted. When we do, Satan rejoices. Today, like every other day, provides countless opportunities to serve God and to worship Him. But, if we turn our backs on our Creator, or if we simply become too busy to acknowledge His greatness, we do a profound disservice to ourselves, to our families, and to our world.

Timeless Wisdom for Godly Living

Men spend their lives in anticipation, in determining to be vastly happy at some period or other, when they have time. But the present time has one advantage over every other: it is ours.

Charles Caleb Colton

A glimpse of the next three feet of road is more important and useful than a view of the horizon.

C. S. Lewis

Encourage one another daily, as long as it is called Today....

Hebrews 3:13 NIV

It has been well said that no man ever sank under the burden of the day. It is when tomorrow's burden is added to the burden of today that the weight is more than a man can bear. Never load yourselves so, my friends. If you find yourselves so loaded, at least remember this: it is your own doing, not God's. He begs you to leave the future to Him and mind the present.

George MacDonald

Wherever you are, be all there.
Live to the hilt every situation you believe to be the will of God.

Jim Elliot

More Words from God's Word

*Give your entire attention to what God is doing right now,
and don't get worked up about what may or may not happen tomorrow.
God will help you deal with whatever hard things come up
when the time comes.*

Matthew 6:34 MSG

*When you and your children return to the LORD your God and obey
him with all your heart and with all your soul according to everything
I command you today, then the LORD your God will restore your fortunes
and have compassion on you and gather you again from
all the nations where he scattered you.*

Deuteronomy 30:2-3 NIV

*You must choose for yourselves today whom you will serve . . .
as for me and my family, we will serve the LORD.*

Joshua 24:15 NCV

My Values for Life

	Check Your Value		
	High	Med.	Low
I understand that today is a precious gift . . .	___	___	___
I trust that the way I choose to live today will have a profound impact on my future . . .	___	___	___
I believe that it is important to live passionately, obediently, and joyfully . . .	___	___	___

Today

First Things First

The thing you should want most is God's kingdom
and doing what God wants.
Then all these other things you need will be given to you.

Matthew 6:33 NCV

On your daily to-do list, all items are not created equal: Certain tasks are extremely important while others are not. Therefore, it's imperative that you prioritize your daily activities and complete each task in the approximate order of its importance.

The principle of doing first things first is simple in theory but more complicated in practice. Well-meaning family, friends, and coworkers have a way of making unexpected demands upon your time. Furthermore, each day has it own share of minor emergencies; these urgent matters tend to draw your attention away from more important ones. On paper, prioritizing is simple, but to act upon those priorities in the real world requires maturity, patience, determination, and balance.

If you fail to prioritize your day, life will automatically do the job for you. So your choice is simple: prioritize or be prioritized. It's a choice that will help determine the quality of your life.

If you're having trouble balancing the many demands of everyday living, perhaps you've been trying to organize your life according to your own plans, not God's. A better strategy, of course, is to take your daily obligations and place them in the hands of the One who created you. To do so, you must prioritize your day according to God's commandments, and you must seek His will and His wisdom in all matters. Then, you can face the coming day with the assurance that the same God who created our universe out of nothingness will help you place first things first in your own life.

Are you living a balanced life that allows time for worship, for family, for work, for exercise, and a little time left over for you? Or do you feel overworked, under-appreciated, overwhelmed, and underpaid? If your to-do list is "maxed out" and your energy is on the wane, it's time to restore a sense of balance to your life. You can do so by turning the concerns and the priorities of this day over to God—prayerfully, earnestly, and often. Then, you must listen for His answer . . . and trust the answer He gives.

Whatever you love most, be it sports, pleasure, business or God, that is your god.

Billy Graham

Values for Life

Making Time for God: Our days are filled to the brim with obligations and priorities, but no priority is greater than our obligation to our Creator. Let's make sure that we give Him the time He deserves, not only on Sundays but also on every other day of the week.

Timeless Wisdom for Godly Living

One hundred years from now it won't matter if you got that big break, or finally traded up to a Mercedes. It *will* greatly matter, one hundred years from now, that you made a commitment to Jesus Christ.

David Shibley

Don't take hold of a thing unless you want that thing to take hold of you.

E. Stanley Jones

First pay attention to me, and then relax.
Now you can take it easy—you're in good hands.

Proverbs 1:33 MSG

No horse gets anywhere until he is harnessed.
No life ever grows great until it is focused, dedicated, disciplined.

Harry Emerson Fosdick

The most important business I'm engaged in ought to be the LORD's business. If it ain't, I need to get off and classify myself and see whose side I'm on.

Jerry Clower

Have you prayed about your resources lately?
Find out how God wants you to use your time and your money.
No matter what it costs, forsake all that is not of God.

Kay Arthur

More Words from God's Word

And I pray this: that your love will keep on growing in knowledge and every kind of discernment, so that you can determine what really matters and can be pure and blameless in the day of Christ.

Philippians 1:9 HCSB

He said to them all, "If anyone desires to come after Me, let him deny himself, and take up his cross daily, and follow Me. For whoever desires to save his life will lose it, but whoever loses his life for My sake will save it."

Luke 9:23-24 NKJV

Let us fix our eyes on Jesus, the author and perfecter of our faith, who for the joy set before him endured the cross, scorning its shame, and sat down at the right hand of the throne of God.

Hebrews 12:2 NIV

My Values for Life

	Check Your Value		
	High	Med.	Low
I understand the importance of reviewing my priorities frequently . . .	___	___	___
On my priority list, I put God first and my family second . . .	___	___	___
I place a high value on doing important tasks first and easy tasks later . . .	___	___	___

Trusting the Creator

It is better to trust the LORD than to put confidence in people.
It is better to trust the LORD than to put confidence in princes.

Psalm 118:8-9 NLT

Do you want to experience a life filled with abundance and peace? If so, here's a word of warning: you'll need to resist the temptation to do things "your way" and commit, instead, to do things God's way.

God has plans for your life. Big plans. But He won't force you to follow His will; to the contrary, He has given you free will, the ability to make decisions on your own. With the freedom to choose comes the responsibility of living with the consequences of the choices you make.

The most important decision of your life is, of course, your commitment to accept Jesus Christ as your personal Lord and Savior. And once your eternal destiny is secured, you will undoubtedly ask yourself this question; "What now, Lord?" If you earnestly seek God's will for your life, you will find it . . . in time.

When you make the decision to seek God's will for your life, you will contemplate His Word, and you will be watchful for His signs. You will associate with fellow believers who will encourage your spiritual growth. And, you will listen to that inner voice that speaks to you in the quiet moments of your daily devotionals.

Sometimes, God's plans are crystal clear, but other times, He leads you through the wilderness before He delivers you to the

Promised Land. So be patient, keep searching, and keep praying. If you do, then in time, God will answer your prayers and make His plans known.

God is right here, and He intends to use you in wonderful, unexpected ways. You'll discover those plans by doing things *His* way . . . and you'll be eternally grateful that you did.

It's been said that when God sends you on a journey,
He will direct your path and light your way, even if it's only one step at a time. And from walking the mountains and valleys of my own life,
I believe that to be true. When the Lord is with me,
I can feel his presence and move out in confidence, and although
I may not know my final destination, I have his assurance
that I'm heading in the right direction.

Al Green

Values for Life

Waiting faithfully for God's plan to unfold is more important than understanding God's plan. Ruth Bell Graham once said, "When I am dealing with an all-powerful, all-knowing God, I, as a mere mortal, must offer my petitions not only with persistence, but also with patience. Someday I'll know why." Even when you can't understand God's plans, you must trust Him and never lose faith!

Timeless Wisdom for Godly Living

When the dream of our heart is one that God has planted there,
a strange happiness flows into us. At that moment,
all of the spiritual resources of the universe are released to help us.
Our praying is then at one with the will of God and becomes
a channel for the Creator's purposes for us and our world.

Catherine Marshall

God is in full control.
Nothing is happening on earth that brings a surprise to heaven.

Charles Swindoll

"I say this because I know what I am planning for you," says the Lord. "I have good plans for you, not plans to hurt you. I will give you hope and a good future."

Jeremiah 29:11 NCV

The one supreme business of life is to find God's plan for your life and live it.

E. Stanley Jones

I find the doing of the will of God leaves me no time
for disputing about His plans.

George MacDonald

More Words from God's Word

It is God who is at work in you, both to will and to work for His good pleasure.

Philippians 2:13 NASB

A man's heart plans his way, but the LORD directs his steps.

Proverbs 16:9 NKJV

Unless the LORD builds a house, the work of the builders is useless.

Psalm 127:1 NLT

You will show me the way of life, granting me the joy of your presence and the pleasures of living with you forever.

Psalm 16:11 NLT

My Values for Life

	Check Your Value		
	High	Med.	Low
Since I trust that God's plans have eternal ramifications, I will seek His will for my life . . .	___	___	___
Since I believe that God has a plan for my day, I set aside quiet time each morning in order to seek His will for my life . . .	___	___	___
My plans are imperfect; God's plans are perfect; so I choose to trust God . . .	___	___	___

God's Plan

The Value of Christ's Sacrifice

But God demonstrates His own love toward us, in that while we were still sinners, Christ died for us.

Romans 5:8 NKJV

On a Friday morning, on a hill at Calvary, Jesus was crucified. Darkness came over the land, the curtain of the temple was torn in two, and finally Jesus called out, "Father, into your hands I commit my spirit" (Luke 23:46 NIV). Christ had endured the crucifixion, and it was finished.

The body of Jesus was wrapped in a linen shroud and placed in a new tomb. It was there that God breathed life into His Son. It was there that Christ was resurrected. It was there that the angels rejoiced. And it was there, that God's plan for the salvation of mankind was made complete.

As we consider Christ's sacrifice on the cross, we should be profoundly humbled and profoundly grateful. And today, as we come to Christ in prayer, we should do so in a spirit of quiet, heartfelt devotion to the One who gave His life so that we might have life eternal.

He was the Son of God, but He wore a crown of thorns. He was the Savoir of mankind, yet He was put to death on a roughhewn cross made of wood. He offered His healing touch to an unsaved world, and yet the same hands that had healed the sick and raised the dead were pierced with nails.

Christ humbled Himself on a cross—for you. He shed His blood—for you. He has offered to walk with you through this life *and* throughout all eternity. As you approach Him today in prayer, think about His sacrifice and His grace. And be humble.

In His humanness, Jesus was a victim, mercilessly hammered to a cross after being spat upon, mocked, and humiliated. But in His deity, He promised the thief on the cross eternal life, as only God can.

John MacArthur

Values for Life

At the foot of the cross, believers gain perspective: Rebecca Manley Pippert writes, " Dust, rusty nails, and blood notwithstanding, the ground at the foot of the cross is the only vantage point from which to view life clearly. To see things there is to see them truly."

Timeless Wisdom for Godly Living

The way of the Cross is no nightmarish death march into oblivion, with just one sacrifice piled on another. It is a straight line to God. It leads home.

Sherwood Eliot Wirt

Ultimately, we cannot understand the full meaning of the cross of Christ. We can only stand in silence before it, acknowledge its wonder, and submit to its power.

Stanley Grenz

Christ did not send me to baptize people but to preach the Good News. And he sent me to preach the Good News without using words of human wisdom so that the cross of Christ would not lose its power.

1 Corinthians 1:17 NCV

There is no detour to holiness. Jesus came to the resurrection through the cross, not around it.

Leighton Ford

The cross means this: Jesus taking our place to satisfy the demands of God's justice and turning aside God's wrath.

James Montgomery Boice

More Words from God's Word

But as for me, I will never boast about anything except the cross of our L*ORD* *Jesus Christ, through whom the world has been crucified to me, and I to the world.*

Galatians 6:14 HCSB

Then He said to them all, "If anyone wants to come with Me, he must deny himself, take up his cross daily, and follow Me."

Luke 9:23 HCSB

Keep your eyes on Jesus, who both began and finished this race we're in. Study how he did it. Because he never lost sight of where he was headed, that exhilarating finish in and with God, he could put up with anything along the way: cross, shame, whatever. And now he's there, in the place of honor, right alongside God.

Hebrews 12:2 MSG

My Values for Life

	Check Your Value		
	High	Med.	Low
I accept the loving act of Jesus on the cross as my way to salvation . . .	___	___	___
I am thankful for the loving gift of my Heavenly Father: the sacrificial gift of His Son Jesus . . .	___	___	___
I bear my cross by being obedient to Jesus . . .	___	___	___

The Gift of Eternal Life

For God so loved the world that He gave His only begotten Son, that whoever believes in Him should not perish but have everlasting life.

John 3:16 NKJV

How marvelous it is that God became a man and walked among us. Had He not chosen to do so, we might feel removed from a distant Creator. But ours is not a distant God. Ours is a God who understands—far better than we ever could—the essence of what it means to be human.

God understands our hopes, our fears, and our temptations. He understands what it means to be angry and what it costs to forgive. He knows the heart, the conscience, and the soul of every person who has ever lived, including you. And God has a plan of salvation that is intended for you. Accept it. Accept God's gift through the person of His Son Christ Jesus, and then rest assured: God walked among us so that you might have eternal life; amazing though it may seem, He did it for you.

As mere mortals, our vision for the future, like our lives here on earth, is limited. God's vision is not burdened by such limitations: His plans extend throughout all eternity. Thus, God's plans for you are not limited to the ups and downs of everyday life. Your Heavenly Father has bigger things in mind . . . much bigger things.

Let us praise the Creator for His priceless gift, and let us share the Good News with all who cross our paths. We return our Father's love by accepting His grace and by sharing His message and His love. When we do, we are blessed here on earth and throughout all eternity.

As you struggle with the inevitable hardships and occasional disappointments of life, remember that God has invited you to accept His abundance, not only for today, but also for all eternity. So keep things in perspective. Although you will inevitably encounter occasional defeats in this world, you'll have all eternity to celebrate the ultimate victory in the next.

The gift of God is eternal life, spiritual life, abundant life through faith in Jesus Christ, the Living Word of God.

Anne Graham Lotz

Values for Life

What a friend you have in Jesus: Jesus loves you, and He offers you eternal life with Him in heaven. Welcome Him into your heart. Now!

Timeless Wisdom for Godly Living

Someday you will read in the papers that Moody is dead. Don't you believe a word of it. At that moment I shall be more alive than I am now. I was born of the flesh in 1837, I was born of the spirit in 1855. That which is born of the flesh may die. That which is born of the Spirit shall live forever.

D. L. Moody

Let us see the victorious Jesus, the conqueror of the tomb, the one who defied death. And let us be reminded that we, too, will be granted the same victory.

Max Lucado

I assure you, anyone who believes in me already has eternal life.

John 6:47 NLT

O Sovereign God! You have humbled yourself in order to exalt us. You became poor so that we might become rich. You came to us so that we can come to you. You took upon yourself our humanity in order to raise us up into eternal life. All this comes through your grace, free and unmerited; all this through your beloved Son, our Lord and Savior, Jesus Christ.

Karl Barth

More Words from God's Word

And this is the testimony: that God has given us eternal life, and this life is in His Son. He who has the Son has life.

1 John 5:11-12 NKJV

For the wages of sin is death, but the gift of God is eternal life in Christ Jesus our Lord.

Romans 6:23 NIV

For the law of the Spirit of life in Christ Jesus has set you free from the law of sin and of death.

Romans 8:2 NASB

For if we believe that Jesus died and rose again, even so God will bring with Him those who sleep in Jesus.

1 Thessalonians 4:14 NKJV

My Values for Life

Statement	Check Your Value: High	Med.	Low
I believe my eternity with God is secure because I believe in Jesus . . .	___	___	___
I have a responsibility to tell as many people as I can about the eternal life that Jesus offers . . .	___	___	___
I praise God and His Son for the gift of eternal life . . .	___	___	___

Values for Life

Therefore whoever hears these sayings of Mine, and does them, I will liken him to a wise man who built his house on the rock: and the rain descended, the floods came, and the winds blew and beat on that house; and it did not fall, for it was founded on the rock.

Matthew 7:24-25 NKJV

Index of Topics